CAESARS PALACE®

THE COMPLETE GUIDE TO
GAMING

CAESARS PALACE ®

THE COMPLETE GUIDE TO GAMING

GPG

General Publishing Group, Inc.
Los Angeles

Publisher: W. Quay Hays
Editorial Director: Peter Hoffman
Editor: Colby Allerton
Art Director: Kurt Wahlner
Writers: Frank Coffey and Joe Layden

Cover photograph © Scott Sandler

Nevada law provides only general standards of conduct for the
operation of licensed games and slot machines. Casinos in
Nevada may set their own rules and may change the rules
from time to time without notice. House rules must be
conspicuously posted in the race and sports book and in any
poker room. In addition, payoff schedules or award cards
applicable to licensed games and slot machines must be
conspicuously displayed at all times, either at or adjacent to
the game or machine.

For information:
General Publishing Group, Inc.
2701 Ocean Park Boulevard
Santa Monica, California 90405

Library of Congress Cataloging-in-Publication Data

Caesars Palace: the complete guide to gaming.
    p. cm.
  ISBN 1-57544-055-5
  1. Gambling.   I. General Publishing Group, Inc.
GV1301.C24   1997
794'.01—dc21   97-12636
                                       CIP

Printed by RR Donnelley & Sons, Inc. in the USA
10 9 8 7 6 5 4 3 2

General Publishing Group, Inc.
Los Angeles

CONTENTS

INTRODUCTION 7

CHAPTER 1
SLOTS 11

CHAPTER 2
ROULETTE 25

CHAPTER 3
CRAPS 37

CHAPTER 4
PAI GOW &
PAI GOW POKER 51

CHAPTER 5
BACCARAT 65

CHAPTER 6
BLACKJACK 81

CHAPTER 7
CARIBBEAN
STUD POKER 95

CHAPTER 8
KENO 103

CHAPTER 9
BIG SIX 117

CHAPTER 10
CAESARS PALACE RACE
& SPORTS BOOK....................123

CHAPTER 11
VIDEO POKER.......................137

AFTERWORD 157

GLOSSARY..............................159

INTRODUCTION

There is no city on earth quite like Las Vegas, and no casino quite like Caesars Palace. Thirty years after the doors opened and the first wave of customers washed over the threshold, Caesars remains the standard against which all other casinos are measured. Ideally situated on the Las Vegas Strip, at the heart of one of the most vibrant and fastest-growing cities in the world, Caesars has something for everyone— from the high roller in town for a serious weekend of big-money baccarat to the casual player who simply wants to enjoy the clean desert air and take a crack at the quarter slot machines. Whatever your tastes, Caesars Palace will satisfy you. That's a promise!

At Caesars, there are more than 2,000 slot machines offering payoffs that exceed $1 million!

A world-class resort famous for its exceptional entertainment, special events, fine dining and luxurious accommodations, Caesars Palace will dazzle you with excitement and, with its wide variety of games of chance, challenge your skill and bravado as a gambler. Las Vegas, after all, is a city whose spectacular rise can be attributed largely to the popularity of the gaming industry. We've never forgotten that at Caesars Palace. And so you'll find our gaming facilities, as always, to be on the cutting edge.

Looking for both quantity and quality? We've got it. State-of-the-art technology and unparalleled service have allowed Caesars Palace to maintain its position as an industry leader. Just look around: There are more than 2,000 slot machines offering payoffs that exceed $1 million! (Our frequent slot customers can also take advantage of the Caesars Emperors Club, which pays off with discounts on shopping and meals, Caesars merchandise and Club Cash, which can be redeemed for additional slot play.) More than 100 tables feature today's most popular games, including blackjack, craps, baccarat, roulette, pai gow poker and Caribbean stud poker—with betting limits that range from $5 to $10,000; 24-hour keno, with the most dedicated and reliable keno runners in the business never more than a few feet away; video versions of just about everything; and, for the true sports fan, the Caesars Palace Race and Sports Book, which offers simulcasting of horse races and athletic events from around the globe—and, of course, the opportunity to wager a few bucks on the outcome.

Caesars Palace offers daily instructional classes in all casino games; an informative, and humorous, instructional video is also available on the in-room cable network.

Caesars has so much to offer the gambling enthusiast that it doesn't all fit into one casino. That's why we have two: the Roman Casino and the Forum Casino, totaling approximately 120,000 square feet of floor space. That's the size of three football fields!

We don't mind if you're impressed by our size, but please don't be intimidated. Caesars Palace prides itself on providing an atmosphere conducive to having fun. We want guests to feel comfortable. And we want them to be equipped with the knowledge necessary to fully enjoy all of the games that are available. People come to Las Vegas for all kinds of reasons—but most want to at least try their hand at gambling. Unfortunately, the unique language and protocol of the blackjack, baccarat and craps tables overwhelm a great many visitors—so much so that they never summon the courage to pull up a chair. We understand their apprehension; at the same time, we want to encourage them to experience the myriad gaming opportunities available. To that end, Caesars Palace offers daily instructional classes in all casino games; an informative, and humorous, instructional video is also available on the in-room cable network.

Guests should also take the time to thoroughly examine this book, which outlines the rules and procedures for the games played at Caesars Palace. We've tried to make the guide as user-friendly as possible, so that even a novice won't feel intimidated. We've taken great care to break down each game into its simplest components, as well as explain the sometimes bewildering jargon commonly heard at the tables. Many casino games seem almost mystifying to the uninitiated. In actuality they're all fairly easy to understand—once you've taken the time to educate yourself.

This book will give you a foundation on which to build your gaming wisdom. Read it. Enjoy it. Use it to your benefit. And when you get to the casino, feel free to ask for more help. After all, the casino personnel—from the dealers and the pit bosses to the cashiers—are there to serve your needs. Part of their job is to make sure that you understand how to play. So don't be shy about asking questions.

Remember, it's your money. So have fun. And good luck!

CHAPTER 1
SLOTS
Machines of Magic

Slot machines have captivated gamblers for more than a century ever since a San Francisco machinist named Charles Fey invented the first one in the 1890s. Fey's machines were sturdy little beasts handcrafted from cast iron, and they soon began showing up in bars and taverns throughout the Bay area.

The Liberty Bell, as the first model was known, quickly acquired a large and devoted following. Although technologically primitive, it operated on the same philosophical principle that drives the slot frenzy of the 1990s: People love the idea of risking a small amount of money for the chance to win a large amount. Customers would sit on their bar stools and pump coins into the Liberty Bell all day, waiting…hoping…for a huge return on their investment. Charles Fey certainly did all right. As did the tavern owners who stocked the Liberty Bell and split profits with Fey, 50-50.

People love the idea of risking a small amount of money for the chance to win a large amount.

Though clunkier and less sophisticated, the Liberty Bell bore a definite physical resemblance to today's slot machines. On the front were three windows through which three different wheels could be viewed. On each of the wheels were 10 different symbols. Some were taken from playing cards (the intent, after all, was to attract customers already familiar with gambling): diamonds, spades, clubs, hearts. Others represented bells, horseshoes and stars. Customers spun the three wheels by pulling a long arm attached to the side of the machine.

The early games were quite simple. A customer inserted a coin into a slot (the minimum amount required for a single play varied—from a nickel to a silver dollar), then pulled the arm and waited, transfixed, while the Liberty Bell worked its magic. Although several rows of symbols were at least partially visible through the machine's windows, only the symbols that lined up across the middle row—or "pay line"—mattered. Payouts were based on a fixed schedule that was printed on each machine, and redeemable in the form of alcohol (the early Liberty Bells, remember, were found almost exclusively in bars). The

The biggest prize, for three bells, was 10 drinks.

smallest prize was one drink, which the player won if he "caught" (slot parlance for hitting the right symbols) two horseshoes. The biggest prize, for three bells, was 10 drinks.

For a time, Fey had a monopoly on the slot-machine business. But in the early 1900s, Herbert Stephen Mills, a businessman who specialized in manufacturing carnival games, obtained one of the Liberty Bells and decided to copy its design. (Patent laws did not then cover devices used for gambling purposes.) He recruited the foreman of Fey's manufacturing operation, went into business for himself, and soon eclipsed Fey as the United States' leading producer of slot machines. It was Mills who designed the layout commonly seen on modern-day slot machines: three wheels clearly visible behind three windows, with symbols that include a variety of fruits—peaches, plums, oranges, cherries, lemons—as well as the bell and bar. Players won prizes if the symbols lined up in certain ways.

Mills also understood the psychological power of the slot machine, which is why he made the windows larger and clearer—so that players could easily see not only the pay line but other rows as well.

You can play for as little as a nickel (still!) a pull, or as much as $500 a pull.

That way, if the row immediately below the pay line revealed a winning combination, the player was teased (tricked, actually) into thinking he had "almost" won. And so he would naturally keep inserting coins into the slot.

It was the notion of teasing that led Mills to invent the first slot-machine "jackpot." In the middle of the machine was another window, through which the player could see a box filled with coins. Each time someone played the machine, a percentage of the coins flowed into the box. And the box continued to swell until someone hit the jackpot—typically represented by three bars. The sight of all that money, of course, kept customers in their seats, yanking on the handle, hoping for some reward.

Speaking of the handle...according to popular legend, the slot machine acquired its infamous moniker in the 1930s, when a judge imposing sentence on a defendant found guilty of running an illegal gambling operation referred to the devices as "one-armed bandits."

Or so the story goes. True or not, it's an appropriate nickname, for slot machines have picked a lot of pockets over the years. Then again, they've also spit out a lot of money. The trick—in 1897 or 1997—is to be in the right place at the right time; to be staring down the one-armed bandit when the bells ring and the sirens scream, and the jackpot light burns bright.

AN ARRAY OF HIGH-TECH MACHINES

Modern technology has changed the slot machine in many ways. Today's slots feature a variety of multiple-coin, multiple-line options. They keep track of credit, and offer video options and progressive payoffs of up to $10 million. You can play for as little as a nickel (still!) a pull, or as much as $500 a pull. Actually, you don't even have to pull. Most machines now offer push-button options, making the traditional lever unnecessary.

But guess what? Casinos operators have discovered that a large percentage of their customers *like* the lever. A few years back, attempts were made to radically alter the machines by removing the handles and replacing the traditional spinning reels with video screens. The response was overwhelmingly negative. So, the vast majority of machines today combine modern technology with traditional aesthetics. Video slot machines are available, but they are in the minority. As we approach the 21st century, the one-armed bandit—reels and all—is still the one-armed

bandit. Whether you use the arm is strictly your choice.

Technology has changed the game in other ways. Virtually all slot machines in operation today are controlled by computer microprocessors, the nerve center of which is a device known as a random number generator. It ensures that slot-machine play is truly "random" by selecting numbers according to a preprogrammed mathematical formula—but with no regard to sequence. The computer chooses from more than four billion numbers, which are then translated into symbols matching the symbols on the slot display. Some of the numbers are winning numbers; some are losing numbers. The percentage of winning numbers varies, depending on how the computer has been programmed.

The numbers are spit out at a mind-boggling rate: several hundred per second. And what many people do not understand is that the process continues even when the machine is not in use. If you walk away from a slot machine to get change, chat with a friend, or for any other reason, the computer continues to work. It grabs numbers, good and bad, whether you're playing or not. What this means, of course, is that there is no such thing as a machine that is "ready" or "due." More than one player has pumped coin after coin into a slot machine and walked away a loser, only to discover minutes later that the very same machine has given up a jackpot to someone else. The losing player feels angry and betrayed—sentiments that, while under-standable, are actually misplaced.

The truth is, because the computer is constantly generating new numbers, winning is a matter of precise timing...and luck. If the aforementioned losing player had remained at the machine for one more pull, or two, or three...or even 50 more pulls, there is no guarantee that he would have won the jackpot snared by the player who followed him. As a matter of fact, unless he had pulled the lever at *precisely* the same moment, he would not have won. That is the way modern, computerized slot machines work. The machine does not pay off after a given number of pulls. It simply pays off—randomly.

HOW TO PLAY

Part of the allure of playing the slots is that they are neither complicated nor particularly expensive. If you have a handful of change, you can walk into a casino, step up to a slot machine, drop in a coin, and pull the handle. And with a little luck, you can walk out a winner.

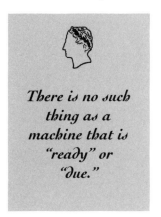

There is no such thing as a machine that is "ready" or "due."

There is virtually no skill attached to playing the slots. You need only a basic understanding of the game and its procedures. The absolute beginner should know that all slot machines have a few things in common: a slot to insert coins; a tray where (if you're really lucky) the coins will land if you hit a winning combination; a glass or plastic display through which you can see the spinning reels; and a handle or button that starts each play.

After you've inserted your coin (or coins), simply pull the handle (or press the button), and hope for the best. The reels soon stop. If the right combination appears on the pay line, the machine pays off. Generally, three of any one symbol is a winning combination, with three bars being best. Some machines, though, pay off on other combinations as well. Each machine should have a payout schedule clearly marked.

As we've said, it takes only a single coin to play the slots. However, virtually all modern slot machines accept multiple coins. (At Caesars Palace, you can wager from one to 10 coins per play, depending on the model you select.) By inserting additional coins (or tokens) you can dramatically expand the parameters of the game. The simplest example of this is the nonprogressive slot machine that accepts multiple coins. On these machines, several payout schedules are posted near the display. They are generally self-explanatory: on a winning play, two coins produce twice as large a payoff as one coin; four coins produce twice as large a payoff as two coins, etc. Simply put, the more coins you play, the more coins you win. If you hit the jackpot, some machines will pay the entire jackpot amount; others require payment from a slot attendant. And there are other options. For example:

The machine does not pay off after a given number of pulls. It simply pays off—randomly.

PROGRESSIVE SLOT MACHINES

Among the most popular casino attractions are progressive machines, which give the player

This photograph depicting IGT products is reproduced with the consent of IGT.

an opportunity to expand the jackpot by playing additional coins. The biggest jackpot in a progressive slot machine continues to swell until somebody hits it. Players seeking the biggest prizes seem to prefer the progressive slots. Grand jackpots at progressive machines can be enormous. Prizes in excess of $100,000 are not uncommon. And some jackpots, which employ several machines linked together electronically, offer jackpots of several million dollars. (Caesars Palace, for instance, once paid three separate $1 million jackpots in a six-month period.)

Granted, the odds against winning such a jackpot are steep. But someone will win. Eventually. And that fact alone is enough to keep the machines humming 24 hours a day. Those playing progressive slots are advised to make sure they're playing the required number of coins on each pull. Otherwise they'll be ineligible for the grand jackpot. Practically speaking, playing progressive slots without inserting the maximum number of coins required for grand-jackpot consideration is a waste of time and money.

MULTIPLE-LINE SLOT MACHINES

On a standard slot machine, players "cash out" only if a winning combination appears in the center pay line. But on a multiple-line machine, players can literally "buy" addition-al pay lines. For exam-ple, inserting one coin displays the center line, but inserting two coins displays the center and top lines; inserting three coins displays the top, center and bottom lines.

But the most practical suggestion is this: Never play just one coin.

This type of machine can be fairly exotic. On the most elaborate multiple-line machines you can purchase virtu-ally every line on the display—including diagonal lines.

STRATEGY

We've already pointed out that winning at slots is largely a matter of luck. There is no particular skill that will give you an advantage when playing against a slot machine. State law in Nevada requires that slot machines return a minimum of 75 percent of the money put into them; most casinos, however, claim a return of 90 to 95 percent. The house advan-tage is generally estimated to be 3 to 25 per-cent (with 4 to 14 percent being average), depending on how the machine has been pro-grammed, the type of game being played and the player's tactical approach.

Tactical approach? In a game of luck? Well, yes. While it's true that fate is the deter-mining factor in a game of slots, there are a few things you can do to improve the odds.

Some are obvious, such as walking away from an unusually stingy machine (one that refuses to give up a cent, even when you've been playing for quite some time). But the most practical suggestion is this: Never play just one coin. Not only will you forfeit grand-jackpot eligibility on progressive machines, but even in straight slots, you'll be throwing away your money. It's been statistically demonstrated that you improve your odds of winning at slots whenever you play the maximum number of coins allowed. So if you want to bet one dollar per pull, forget about playing the dollar slot machine; you're better off inserting four quarters into a 25-cent slot.

Prizes in excess of $100,000 are not uncommon. And some jackpots, which employ several machines linked together electronically, offer jackpots of several million dollars.

JOIN THE CLUB

Most casinos offer special benefits to players who join their slot clubs. At Caesars Palace, the frequent player is strongly advised to join the Emperors Club. By using the Emperors Club Card when you play slots (quarter denomination or higher) at Caesars, you will earn points toward Club Cash, special Caesars merchandise, and other benefits and privileges (including discounts on meals, shows and rooms).

You can pick up a courtesy introductory card by stopping at the Club Booth in either the Roman Casino or Forum Casino. Simply insert the card in the reader box attached to the slot machine, and begin the countdown toward your first point. When the countdown reaches zero, you've earned one point. Earn 20 points in three days, and you'll receive special discounts, a gift and your personal membership card.

If you like playing the slots, you'll love the Emperors Club!

CHAPTER 2
ROULETTE
Where the Ball Stops...
And Where It Started

Roulette is one of the world's oldest casino games. The word "roulette" comes from the French *roue*, loosely translated as "wheel." Of course, anyone remotely familiar with gaming knows that the two basic components of roulette are a wheel and a ball. The object of the game, in simplest terms, is to predict where the ball will land on the spinning roulette wheel.

The history of roulette can be traced back to ancient Greece, where soldiers played a version of the game by spinning a shield on the point of a sawed-off sword and betting on where the shield would stop. Julius Caesar even had a chariot wheel installed in the gaming room of his imperial palace; by spinning the wheel on a vertical axle in the floor, he was able to play another version of roulette.

Today, the swords, shields and chariot wheels favored by Caesar and his contemporaries have been eliminated, but the spirit of the game remains intact. Indeed, the excitement of roulette has endured the passing of several centuries. According to some historians, the modern version of roulette has its roots in 17th-century France, where mathematician (and philosopher!) Blaise Pascal, during a monastic retreat in Paris, invented the game. Others claim Pascal was merely conducting experiments with a ball and wheel, and though he may have named his "invention" *roulette*, he never thought of it as a game— let alone one for the casino. That people might be interested in betting on the outcome of such a game was, presumably, of little concern to Pascal. Others exploited this potential.

That is but one theory. Other historians believe roulette was created by a French monk to help fight the drudgery of life in the monastery. And still others compare it to an ancient Chinese game whose object was to arrange statuettes in a particular order; some years later, a group of French Dominican monks combined the statuettes with a revolving wheel to form the first game of roulette.

Or so the story goes. This much is known for certain: The first roulette wheels intended specifically for gambling purposes were introduced in the early 18th century in European casinos. The game was known as *hoca*, and eventually it spawned a variety of wheel-and-ball games, including *petits chevaux*, E.O. (Even-Odd), *boule* and, ultimately, the game we know today as roulette.

HOW TO PLAY

Roulette is a quiet, simple game. Players stand or sit at a table while a dealer spins the wheel and ball and waits for it to fall into one of the numbered slots on the wheel. Your job, as a player, is to guess where the ball will land. Generally, roulette is not a game that requires great skill; it is a game of luck. However, despite the leisurely pace (watching the ball spin one way while the wheel spins another, and waiting for the inevitable drop, is an almost hypnotic experience), it can be a thrilling game, for the payoff is sometimes extraordinary—as high as 35-1 for the player who places, and wins, the most daring bet!

THE WHEEL

The focus of all attention in roulette is the wheel itself. Roughly three feet in diameter and weighing, on average, nearly 100 pounds, the wheel features 38 numbers, each in its own neat little individual compartment. The numbers are 1 through 36, along with 0 and 00. The wheel is laid out in such a way that 18 of the numbers are black and 18 are red. The 0 and 00 are both green. Black and red numbers alternate—with two notable exceptions: 0 is flanked by a pair of black numbers; 00 is flanked by a pair of red numbers. Numbers do not follow a typical "counting" progression around the wheel (1-2-3-4-5-6); rather, pairs of even numbers alternate with pairs of odd numbers.

Roulette is not a game that requires great skill; it is a game of luck. Despite the leisurely pace, it can be a thrilling game.

(The exception, again, are those numbers adjacent to 0 and 00, which, as we will discuss in greater detail, are the numbers that make roulette such a challenging game for the player, and such a profitable game for the house.) At Caesars, we also provide several single 0 wheels that reduce the house advantage by approximately half. These wheels have a different order of numbers.

After all bets are placed, the dealer releases a small plastic ball onto a track at the upper portion of the wheel. As the wheel spins in a counterclockwise direction, the ball spins clockwise. When the ball begins to slow down, it will leave the track and land in one of the 38 numbered slots, but not before encountering some turbulence in the form of small metal buffers strategically placed around the wheel. The buffers add a touch of excitement to the game's final seconds and help ensure a thoroughly random result. These buffers are

sometimes referred to as "canoes" due to their shape.

When the ball finally comes to rest in one of the compartments, the dealer calls out the winning number, collects from all losers and pays off all winners.

THE CHIPS

One of the first things you'll notice when you approach a game of roulette is that it is played with special chips. Each player uses a different-color chip so that the dealer can keep track of all bets. Color is no indication of chip value, and a player can dictate how much chips are worth. For this reason, roulette chips should never leave the game. This system is used in roulette and not in other casino games because of the extraordinarily broad range of betting possibilities. Eleven different types of bets can be placed in roulette, in 150 different combinations. Many players make random bets, scattering chips all over the table. Color-coding just makes the dealer's job a little easier. After a few spins of the wheel, you'll get used to it.

When you arrive at the table, you will have to purchase roulette chips. When you leave the table, the dealer will convert your roulette chips into casino chips; if you want cash, you'll have to visit the cashier's window.

THE TABLE

All bets in roulette are made by placing chips on a table located near the wheel. Printed on the table is a layout of the numbers found on the roulette wheel. The numbers are arranged in a large rectangle: three long vertical columns, each containing 12 numbers. At the bottom of each column are small boxes bearing the words "2 to 1." By placing a chip in one of those boxes, you are betting on all of the numbers in that column. If the ball lands on any of those numbers, you are a winner, and your wager will be rewarded at 2-1 odds.

To the immediate left of the columns of numbers are three smaller boxes. The first reads "1st 12," the second reads "2nd 12" and the third, as you might expect, reads "3rd 12." By placing a chip on one of these boxes you are betting on either the first, second or third dozen numbers on the roulette wheel—in sequence (1 through 12, 13 through 24, or 25 through 36). This bet also pays 2-1 odds.

To the left of these boxes are six more boxes reflecting other types of bets: "1 to 18," "19 to 36," "Odd," "Even," "Red," "Black." Most of these are self-explanatory. If you place a chip on the word "Red," for example, you are betting that the ball will land on one of the red numbers. If you place a chip on "1 to 18," you are betting that the ball will land on any of the first 18 numbers.

Finally, at the top of the three long columns of numbers are the numbers 0 and 00.

PLACING YOUR BET

Okay, you've made it to the table, watched a few spins of the wheel and exchanged cash or casino chips for roulette chips. Now you're ready to play. But where do you begin? Well, that's up to you. The great thing about roulette is that the possibilities seem almost limitless. You can make a bet that pays even money, or you can take your chances on a 35-1 shot. Or you can make both plays on a

single spin of the wheel. Many roulette players often place several different types of bets,
which makes the game more exciting.

Roulette is not a complicated game. There
are two basic categories of wagers: straight bets
(in which you place your chip on any of the
spaces described above) and combination
bets (such as a "split," "trio" or "corner"). The
payoffs on these bets vary, and the method
for placing the bet is quite
precise (though not com-
plicated), so let's take a
look at each.

Straight-up: This is
a single-number bet on
any number (including
0 and 00). For instance,
you place a chip on the
number 22. If the wheel
stops on that number,
you win. This bet pays
35-1 odds and is the
longest shot in the game.

Split: This is any
two adjoining numbers
(including 0 and 00). To
place this bet, simply position your chip in such a
way that it covers the line
separating the two numbers. For example,
you'd like to place a split bet on 17 and 20,
which are juxtaposed on the roulette table.
Just place a chip on the line between those
two numbers. If the wheel stops on either 17
or 20, you win. This bet pays 17-1.

Street: A street bet is a three-number bet.
Also known as a "trio," this bet is made by
placing your chip on the edge of a horizontal
row of numbers. For example, if you want

Eleven different types of bets can be placed in roulette, in 150 different combinations. Many players make random bets, scattering chips all over the table.

to place a street bet on 7-8-9, place your chip (or chips) on the outside edge of the seven. This covers all three numbers and pays off at 11-1 odds.

Five-number bet: There is only one type of five-number bet: one that covers 0-00-1-2-3. To place this bet, place your chip on the line above the number 2. If the ball lands on any of these five numbers, your bet is rewarded at 6-1 odds.

Line: A line bet is a wager on six consecutive numbers, such as 13-14-15-16-17-18. Make this bet by placing your chip on the outside line separating two rows (between the 15 and 18, for example). If any of your six numbers comes up a winner, you will be paid at 5-1 odds.

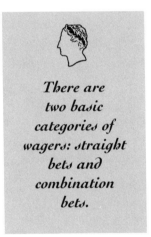

There are two basic categories of wagers: straight bets and combination bets.

Dozen: This is a bet on the first, second or third dozen numbers (1-12, 13-24 or 25-36). To make this bet, place your chip on the spaces marked "1st 12," "2nd 12" or "3rd 12." A winning dozen bet pays 2-1 odds.

Corner: Also known as a "square," the corner bet gives you four adjoining numbers, such as 1, 2, 4, 5. To make this bet, place your chip at the point where the four numbers converge. A winning corner bet pays 8-1.

Column: As the name implies, a column bet includes all 12 numbers in a single column, such as 1-4-7-10-13-16-19-22-25-28-31-34. To place this bet, position your chip on the space marked "2 to 1" at the bottom of a particular column of numbers. A winning column bet pays 2-1.

High/low: A high/low bet is a wager on either the first 18 or last 18 numbers on the wheel (0 and 00 are losing numbers in this bet). If you'd like to bet on 1 through 18, place your chip on the space marked "1 to 18." If you'd like to bet on 19 through 36, place your chip on the space marked "19 to 36." A winning high/low bet pays even money.

Odd/even: This is exactly as it sounds: betting on all of the odd numbers or all of the even numbers (not including 0 and 00, which, again, are losing numbers). To place a bet on even numbers, put your chip on the space marked "Even." To place a bet on odd numbers, put your chip on the space marked "Odd." Winning bets pay even money.

Red/black: This is another very simple bet. Choose a color and position your chips accordingly. If you want to bet on all of the black numbers, place your chip on the space marked "Black." If you'd like to bet on all of the red numbers, place your chip on the space marked "Red" (0 and 00, which are green, are losing numbers). A red/black bet pays even money.

You can tailor the game to your taste by combining any or all of these bets. Roulette can be sublimely simple or highly exotic. It's your call. As long as you understand these basic bets, you'll be prepared for anything.

THE ODDS

You can win big in roulette. Pick the right number and that $10 bet becomes $360! Wagering can be relatively safe (black/red, odd/even) or extremely risky (straight-up). Remember, though, that roulette is among the casino's most challenging games. There are no effective mathematical "systems" to help guide your wagering. Roulette is strictly a game of chance, albeit an exciting one. Keep in mind, too, that the house owns an advantage of 5.26 percent. That doesn't mean you can't win; it simply means you'll have to *earn* your money.

ETIQUETTE

As we've already noted, roulette is a leisurely game. Players have plenty of time to place their bets. You should keep a couple of things in mind, however.

• Always place your chips carefully. Combination bets require players to position their chips in precisely the right place. If you make a mistake, and put your chip on the wrong line, you will be held accountable. Dealers don't accept excuses.

• Make sure that you follow the dealer's instructions. When the dealer calls for bets, place yours.

• At Caesars, we allow a player to continue betting once the ball has been released onto the track, and approximately four rotations prior to the ball leaving the track and bouncing into the slot, the dealer will announce "no more bets," waving his hand over the layout.

CHAPTER 3
CRAPS
Dice of Life

Craps is the fastest and most exciting casino game. To the uninitiated, it's also the most intimidating. The layout is complex, the action hot, the noise incessant. More than any other casino game, craps encourages its participants to become involved, to have fun—to act as if they are *playing.*

Not that the craps aficionado doesn't take his game seriously; on the contrary—because the game moves so quickly, and because so many different combinations of bets can be placed, an extraordinary amount of money can be won or lost in a very short period of time at the craps table. So it is serious business indeed.

But craps is also a communal game infused with the spirit and passion of the people who are playing. The cool restraint so obviously encouraged at the baccarat, blackjack or poker tables is thoroughly out of place at the craps table. Here, the players yell, curse, cheer and sweat. They pat each other on the back as if they are teammates— and in a sense, they are. You can spend hours at a blackjack table and never acknowledge the existence of the person seated to your left. Rest assured, that will never happen in a game of craps. You are engaged in a ritual whose roots can be traced back more than 20 centuries. (Dice, after all, have been used as instruments of gambling since the time of Caesar; the American version of craps was born in the early 19th century in Louisiana, and is generally acknowledged to be a variation of the English game known as "hazard," which the French sometimes referred to as "craps.") Protocol dictates that you become fully involved in the experience—whether you are winning or losing.

So, go ahead. Loosen that tie. Stretch those vocal cords. The craps table awaits.

HOW TO PLAY

While craps can be a complicated game, it doesn't have to be. In fact, if you concentrate on the most basic wagers (and, statistically speaking, this is sound advice), the game is actually fairly simple. When you first arrive at the craps table, don't be put off by the atmosphere. Players will be shouting, perhaps using jargon that sounds foreign; chips will be moving in all directions; dice will be flying every 30 seconds. It's disorienting at first, but if you take the time to learn the fundamentals, you'll do just fine. And you really *should* take the time (most casinos, including Caesars Palace, offer free lessons), because craps is simply too much fun to miss.

THE SETUP

Each craps table is run by three dealers, along with a "boxman." Two of the dealers stand behind the table, taking bets, paying off winners and raking in chips from losers; each dealer runs half the table. In the middle of the table, directly opposite these two dealers, is a third casino employee known as the "stickman." The name stems from the fact that he uses a stick to retrieve the dice after they've been rolled. The stickman's duties include passing the dice to the "shooter" and dictating the pace of the game. He's also responsible for ensuring that no one has tampered with the dice. The fourth casino employee, the boxman, oversees the three dealers and supervises all of the action.

THE GAME

After all bets have been placed (the various types of bets are presented below), the stickman will push several sets of dice to the shooter. The shooter selects two dice and tosses them along the surface of the table; to ensure a fair roll, the dice must be thrown hard enough to bounce off the wall at the far end of the table. The shooter retains control of the dice until he rolls a 7—or until a decision has been made on the point.

The cool restraint so obviously encouraged at the baccarat, blackjack or poker tables is thoroughly out of place at the craps table.

The exception to this rule, however, is the first roll of the dice. Known as the "come-out," the first roll is very important. If the shooter throws a 7 or 11 on the come-out, he is an automatic winner and retains control of the dice. If the come-out roll is a 2, 3 or 12—all known as "craps"—he is an automatic loser. He does, however, keep possession of the dice, because he has not yet rolled a 7. Confused? Don't be. It gets easier.

If the shooter rolls a 4, 5, 6, 8, 9 or 10 on the come-out roll, that number becomes the "point." The dealers then place a marker (known as a "puck") in the corresponding box on the craps layout, signifying to all of the players at the table that a point has been established. From this moment, the shooter's objective is to roll this number again—or "make the point"—before he rolls a 7. Everyone else at the table makes wagers based on whether they believe the shooter will accomplish his goal. And that's all there is to it.

For example, let's say you're the shooter. You roll a 4. Your job now is to roll another 4 before you roll a 7. There is no limit to the number of times you are allowed to toss the dice. If it takes you a dozen attempts to roll a 4, that's all right—as long as you don't roll a 7 first. Once you hit the point, the game begins anew, with another come-out roll. You retain control of the dice (in other words, you continue to be the shooter) until you "seven out."

HOW TO BET

Again, betting on craps can be an intensely complicated matter. The layout alone, offering dozens of exotic and combination bets, is enough to bewilder the novice player. But don't be put off. Nearly 90 percent of all craps players restrict their play to the most easily understood types of wagers. You probably should, too.

Line bets: The most basic bet in craps is one involving the "pass line" and "don't pass line," each of which is clearly marked on the layout. This bet is made prior to the come-out roll, and it works like this: If you place your chips on the pass line, you are betting that the come-out roll will be a 7, an 11 or a point number; if the come-out roll is a point number, you are betting that the shooter will hit the point before rolling a 7. In other words, you're betting on the shooter.

A "don't pass" bet is exactly the opposite of a pass bet: You are betting that the come-out roll will be a 2, 3 or 12; or, in the event that the come-out roll establishes a point, you are betting that the shooter will seven out before hitting the point. In other words, a don't pass bet is a bet *against* the shooter.

If the shooter rolls a 2 or 3 on the come-out, the dealers collect the chips of any player who has bet on the pass line, and pay off anyone who has bet on the don't pass line; if the shooter rolls 12 on the come-out, no money changes hands on a don't pass bet.

Come/don't come: One of the most appealing things about craps is that players can make bets as the game progresses, for example, the "come" and "don't come" bets, which are no more complex than line bets. In fact, a come bet is really nothing more than a pass bet that has been placed after the shooter establishes a point. To make a come bet, simply place your chips in the space marked "come" on the craps layout. Typically, come bets are made by players who have already bet on the pass line and are looking to compound their winnings—or losses, as the case may be.

Let's look at a typical come bet. Say the shooter rolls a 5 on his come-out roll. His point number is now 5. If you place a come bet, the next roll of the dice becomes your "come number." For example, let's say the shooter's next throw produces a 4. The dealer will then place your chips on the space marked "4." The game now proceeds exactly as it does on a pass bet. If the shooter rolls another 4 before he rolls a 7, you win your come bet; if he goes seven out, you lose your bet; if the shooter makes his point (in this case, 5), your bet is a "push," and no money changes hands. As in a pass bet, if the first roll of the dice (after you place your come bet) is a 7 or 11, you win immediately. If the first roll is a 2, 3 or 12, you lose immediately.

A don't come bet, as you might expect, is exactly the opposite of a come bet. It is a bet against the shooter. Just as a come bet is played like a pass line bet, a don't come bet is played like a don't pass bet. After a point has been established, you place your chips in the space marked "don't come." If the shooter's next roll is a 7 or 11, you lose automatically. If the next roll is a 2 or 3, you win. A 12, again, is a push. If the shooter's next roll is a 4, 5, 6, 8, 9 or 10, then that is your don't come number. A don't come wager means you are betting that the shooter will seven out before hitting the don't come point. If he rolls a 7, you win; if he hits the point, you lose.

Betting the Odds: "Odds bets" (also known as "behind-the-line" bets, or "free odds" bets) are not even marked on the table, but they are widely considered to be among the best bets a craps player can make.

Line bets and come/don't come bets pay off at even money. If you place a $10 bet on the shooter and he makes his point, you win $10. The house has a modest 1.4 percent advantage on either of these bets, which is one reason why craps should be at the top of every serious gambler's list. Small as that advantage is, you can reduce it even further by placing an odds bet in addition to your original wager.

The odds bet is paid off at the true odds of the number rolled. The house does not pad its edge on the odds bet, which makes it an appealing wager. Of course, in order to place an odds bet, you must first place a line bet or a come/don't come bet. The odds bet enables the house to generate more action and more money in the long run;

When you first arrive at the craps table, players will be shouting, perhaps using jargon that sounds foreign; dice will be flying every 30 seconds.

in the short run, however, it allows you—the player—to have more than just a sporting chance; it allows you to play a game in which the house's advantage dips below 1 percent— the lowest of any game in the casino.

Here's how to play the odds bet. Let's say you make a $10 wager on the pass line, and the shooter rolls a 10. The actual odds against rolling a 10 are 2-1. So, if you then place a

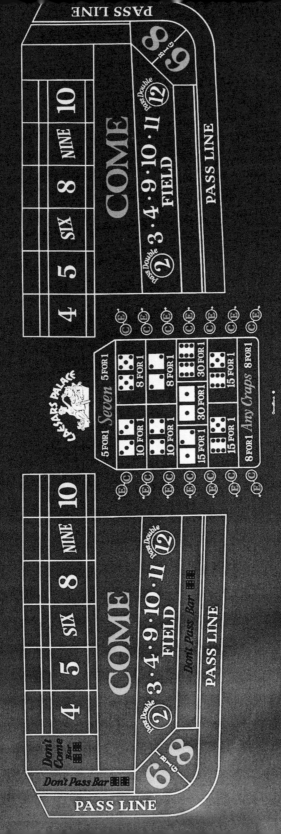

$10 odds bet along with your $10 pass line bet, and the shooter rolls another 10 before rolling a 7, you win two bets. The first pass line bet pays off at even money. But the second bet (the odds bet) pays off at 2-1. That means you win $20 on a $10 bet!

Playing the odds bet on a come bet is no different from playing the odds bet on a pass line bet. You need only keep in mind the true odds of the numbers you are playing. They are as follows:

Point	Odds
4, 10	2-1
5, 9	3-2
6, 8	6-5

According to this chart, a winning $5 odds bet on the number 5 would pay $7.50; however, craps tables do not have 50-cent chips. So, make your bets in the appropriate denominations: Odds bets on 5 and 9 should be an even number ($6, $8), while odds bets on 6 or 8 should be in multiples of $5. Since the 4 and 10 pay off at 2-1 odds, you may place any bet you like.

To take the odds on a pass line wager, you must first bet the pass line. After a point is established, place your additional wager behind the original pass line bet and say "Odds." To take the odds on a come bet, place your chips on the table for the come bet and wait for the dealer to move them into the come number box. Then hand him additional chips and say "Odds" (or, if you like, "Take the odds"). To avoid confusion, you might want to state the point number and the precise amount of your wager. For example, let's say you want to make a $5 odds bet on a point of 6. You would put a $5 chip on the table and say to the dealer, "Five odds six." Knowing exactly what you want, the dealer will then place the second wager almost on top of the first wager. In this way, he'll remember that you have made two wagers: a come bet and an odds bet.

The shooter selects two dice and tosses them along the surface of the table; to ensure a fair roll, the dice must be thrown hard enough to bounce off the wall at the far end of the table.

Note: There are limits on odds bets, and they vary from casino to casino. All casinos allow single-odds bets (in which the odds bet matches the original wager); many permit double-odds wagers (in which the odds bet is twice the original wager). Finding triple odds, five-times odds or 10-times odds, though, is difficult. The reason: To a savvy player, the odds bet represents a way to beat the house. The larger the odds bet, the smaller the house advantage.

You can also place an odds bet on a don't pass or don't come bet. In both cases, though, you will be *laying* rather than *taking* the odds. The procedure for placing these bets is the same. Because the odds are in your favor, though, you must wager more money to win less. Let's say you make a $5 don't pass bet, and the shooter rolls a 10 on the come-out. You then lay the odds. You are betting against the shooter. In this scenario, you have six ways to win and only three ways to lose.

Therefore, if the shooter "craps out" (rolls a 7 before hitting his point), you will have had to wager an additional $10 to win $5 on the odds bet.

STRATEGIES

You don't have to be a genius to realize that craps offers the gambler some of the best odds in the house. Even if you play nothing but the easiest, least-sophisticated bets, you stand a far better chance of winning than you do at the slot machine or roulette wheel—or at just about any other game. And if you take the odds on a regular basis, you can actually find yourself in a nearly fair fight (which is something rare indeed in casino gambling). For that reason alone, you should take the time to learn the basics of craps.

The shooter's objective is to "hit the point" before he rolls a 7. Everyone else at the table makes wagers based on whether they believe the shooter will hit the point.

On the other hand, there are many opportunities to throw your money away at the craps table. As we've already pointed out, the craps layout is almost byzantine in its complexity. In the center of the table are many long-shot opportunities bearing such bizarre names as "hardways bets," "one roll bets" and "horn bets high." These are bets in which the house advantage can be extremely high, and you are advised to stay away from them. If you want to play a long shot, try the keno lounge.

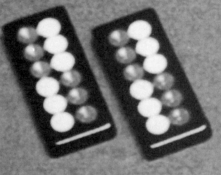

CHAPTER 4
PAI GOW
&
PAI GOW
POKER
Dice of the Ancients

Pai gow is an exciting and challenging game that has tantalized bettors for more than 900 years. Although the game has only recently enjoyed widespread popularity in American casinos, it has long been a favorite among astute Asian players.

Pai gow (pronounced pie gow) is an ancient Chinese version of dominoes, but the game really has as much in common with baccarat and blackjack as it does with the American game of dominoes. The game is believed to have originated in China in the 12th century. The name *pai gow* means, quite literally, "to make nine." That should tell you something about the object of the game.

Part of pai gow's appeal stems from the fact that it combines the skill of traditional card games, such as blackjack, with an esoteric language and a style all its own. Most people, after all, know something about playing blackjack; and virtually everyone knows something about dominoes. Pai gow is another game altogether. To the novice, in fact, the game may seem almost cryptic. Stay with it, though, and you're likely to get hooked, for few casino games combine skill and luck in such equal proportions.

The first thing you should know is that in pai gow, not everything

To the novice, in fact, pai gow may seem almost cryptic. Stay with it, though, and you're likely to get hooked, for few casino games combine skill and luck in such equal proportions.

The Pai Gow Ranking Chart

Pair Rankings "Bo"

Single Rankings

is as it seems. The game is played on a table similar in design to that of a blackjack table: A dealer stands on one side of the table; up to seven players sit or stand on the other side. Instead of cards, the dealer distributes dominoes. The game involves 32 dominoes (or "tiles"), which are mixed (or "shuffled") by the dealer, who then places four dominoes in each of eight individual stacks. The stacks are then distributed to each position at the table—even vacant positions, so that each position receives a stack of tiles.

The first time you watch a game of pai gow, you'll probably be more than a bit confused. For, unlike the American game of dominoes, in pai gow, the value of each tile is *not* based on the numbers of dots that appear on its face. Rather, its value is based on a symbolic Chinese meaning. (Don't worry—you don't have to understand the meaning in order to play the game.) So, while pai gow's translation is "to make nine," it isn't a nine that any aficionado of dominoes would recognize. For example, the best hand in pai gow is a pair, but the best pair is not a pair at all. It's the 1-2 tile (one red dot, two white dots) combined with the 2-4 tile (two white dots, four red dots), both of which are "wild" dominoes. Both can be counted as either 3 or 6, and together they form pai gow's highest hand, known as a "gee joon."

If you've never played pai gow, of course, this probably sounds bizarre. The veteran

Highest pair-ranking tiles "Gee Joon"

player, though, is always on the lookout for either of the wild dominoes, because they are invaluable in strengthening a hand. The novice pai gow player is advised to refer to a pai gow ranking chart until he becomes thoroughly familiar with the numerical rankings. Use the chart in this book or refer to "The Games of Caesars," a brochure that is available throughout the casino. Feel free to bring the chart to the table and to use it after your hand has been dealt; the dealer will understand. Pai gow is an intricate game. It's important that you learn how to play properly and efficiently; until then, take your time and refer to the ranking chart as often as you like.

Unlike the American game of dominoes, in pai gow, the value of each tile is not based on the numbers of dots that appear on its face.

PLAYING THE GAME

Three dice are rolled to determine which position at the table receives the first hand. The counting always begins with the banker (who is not necessarily the dealer—more about that in a minute). If the dice total 9 or 17, then the banker receives the first stack of dominoes. Dealing proceeds counterclockwise, so the player on the banker's right receives the second stack, and so on. If the dice total 10 or 18, then the player to the banker's immediate right receives the first stack of tiles (the banker, of course, receives the last stack).

Pai gow is a rotating bank game. This means that every player has an opportunity to bank the bets against all other players, including the house dealer. In baccarat, when a player serves as a banker, the term is merely ceremonial. In pai gow, however, it is quite literal. To act as the banker, a player must have played the previous hand against the house and must be able to cover all bets. If that seems a bit daunting, fear not. If you prefer, you can choose to have the house act as your co-banker. In that scenario, you would have to cover half the bets. If you do decide to co-bank, you'll have no flexibility in arranging your tiles. Instead, the dealer will arrange your tiles, and you'll be compelled to play the hand according to house rules. You should also know that the house takes a 5 percent commission on each winning hand. The bank rotates counterclockwise. Each player has the option to accept the bank or pass it on to the next player; if no one accepts the bank, it returns to the dealer.

Feel free to bring your ranking chart to the table and to use it after your hand has been dealt; the dealer will understand. Pai gow is an intricate game.

Playing pai gow really isn't that difficult—even if you can't spot a gee joon right away. After all of the tiles have been distributed, each player uses his dominoes to form two separate hands—each, of course, containing two dominoes. The best of the two hands is called the "high hand." The other is called the "low hand." If your high hand ranks higher than the banker's high hand, and your low hand is also higher than the banker's low hand, congratulations! You're an instant winner. If both of your hands rank lower than the banker's hands, sorry, you're an instant loser. And, it follows, if one of your hands is better than the banker's hand, and the other is worse, then the game is considered a tie (also known as a push or standoff), and no money is exchanged. If you and the banker match rankings in both the high hand and low hand, then the hand with the higher "single-ranking" domino is declared the winner.

If the two hands are identical, the banker always wins.

To understand all of this, you'll obviously have to refer to the pai gow ranking chart. Even a cursory glance will tell you that pai gow differs greatly from traditional dominoes. For example, as you can see from the chart, the highest single-ranking domino is one with a face value of 12: three red dots and three

Highest single-ranking tile **Second highest single-ranking tile**

white dots on the top, and three white dots and three red dots on the bottom. Makes sense, right? But look again. The second highest single ranking domino has a face value of only 2: one red dot on the top, one red dot on the bottom.

The best hand is a pair (called a *Bo* in Chinese). But, as already noted, in pai gow, some pairs aren't really pairs; they are merely combinations referred to as pairs. Remember,

Second highest pair-ranking tiles "Bo"

the highest-ranking pair is the gee joon. The second highest-ranking pair, however, really is a pair—an identical pair, in fact. Known as a "teen," it is two 12-spot dominoes. Again, you'll have to refer to the pai gow ranking chart to fully understand the system, and to see if you have one of the "chop" (mixed) pairs.

After a pair, the next best hand is a "wong," which is the 9 domino combined with either a 2 domino or a 12 domino. Only

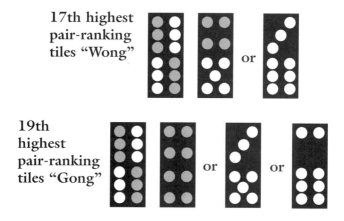

17th highest pair-ranking tiles "Wong"

19th highest pair-ranking tiles "Gong"

a pair can beat a wong. Following the wong in order of importance is the "gong," which is an 8 domino, together with either a 2 or a 12. If you're dealt a poor hand and are unable to make any of these combinations, you must attempt to arrange your dominoes in such a way that each hand approaches or equals 9. Here, as in baccarat, only the last digit is counted. In other words, if you combine a 7 domino with a 6 domino, the value of the hand would be three, not 13.

STRATEGY

As you can see, a high degree of skill is involved in pai gow. You must know how to form the best possible hands, using the four dominoes you've been dealt. So you must be familiar with the pai gow ranking chart. There are, however, a few basic guidelines you should follow.

Play the pairs: Look for pairs first—the gee joon, 11 identical pairs and four mixed pairs. If you find any of these, play them as your high hand.

Gongs, wongs and high 9s: Play a 12 or a 2 with a 7, 8 or 9 to produce either a "high 9," a gong or a wong. These are common, but very strong, high hands.

Think small: Play two small dominoes that add up to a regular 9; if that isn't possible, shoot for 8 or 7. Remember, if you have no pairs, the object is to get as close as you can to 9.

The law of averages: No pairs? No 9s? Then average the hands by playing the biggest domino with the smallest. This is a last resort. If you have nothing else, always play a balanced hand.

The thrill of pai gow (in addition to winning) is in solving what amounts to a puzzle. It is a competitive game that requires intelligence and, obviously, luck. If, however, you become confused while playing, and even a thorough examination of the pai gow ranking chart fails to enlighten you, feel free to ask the dealer or floor supervisor for assistance. Either will be glad to help set your hand.

PAI GOW POKER: OLD MEETS NEW

Pai gow poker—sometimes known as Asian poker—is an odd but compelling mix of the traditional dice game and two types of poker: American five-card stud and high-low. (This section will cover only the nuances of pai gow poker; for a more detailed overview of poker, please see Chapter 11.) It is rapidly becoming one of the most popular casino games.

The dealer shakes the dice cup; as in pai gow, this is merely a ceremony used to determine which player has the honor of receiving the first hand.

Pai gow poker is played with an ordinary deck of 52 cards, plus one joker. The joker is a wild card with limited muscle: It must be used as an ace or to complete a straight or a flush. The object of the game, as in pai gow, is to form the two strongest hands possible based on the cards you are dealt.

PLAYING THE GAME

After the dealer shuffles the deck and calls for bets, he will distribute seven stacks of cards, with seven cards in each stack. He then shakes the dice cup; as in pai gow, this is merely a ceremony used to determine which player has the honor of receiving the first hand. The dice are totaled and the dealer counts counterclockwise from the "chung," a marker that indicates who the banker is. The banker is always counted as number 1, 8 or 15.

As in pai gow, any player may serve as the banker. The only stipulation is that you must be able to cover every wager on the table. If you act as the banker, the other players will be competing directly against you, comparing their hands with your hand—rather than the dealer's hand. When you serve as the banker, the house will wager an amount equal to your bet on the previous hand. If you do not want to be the banker, simply decline the offer; the next player at the table will then be given an opportunity. If no one accepts the role of banker, it returns to the house.

After the cards are distributed, the players arrange their seven cards into two separate hands: one with five cards, the other with two. The hand with five cards is known as the high hand; the hand with two cards, which you might expect to be called the low hand, is actually known as the second highest hand. (Pai gow, like all poker, is an optimist's game.) Once the hands have been arranged, the cards are placed face-down on the table, in the positions indicated on the table's layout.

If you act as the banker, the other players will be competing directly against you, comparing their hands with your hand— rather than the dealer's hand.

To play pai gow, you should have some knowledge of poker. With that knowledge, the game becomes relatively simple, because traditional poker rankings (with one notable exception, which we'll discuss) are used to determine the value of each hand. One rule you must keep in mind, however, is this: The second highest hand must contain only two cards, and must be a lower-ranking hand than the hand containing five cards. For example, let's say the best hand you can muster out of your seven cards is a pair of jacks. You must use that pair in your high hand; you cannot use it as your second highest hand. If this requirement is not met, your hand will be declared a "foul hand," and your wager will be automatically forfeited.

In order to win, your high hand must beat the house's high hand, and your second highest hand must beat the house's second highest hand.

After all the players arrange their hands, the dealer will set the house's hand according to Caesars "house ways." (The house, in other words, has no options.) The outcome is determined by comparing the players' hands with the house's hand (or the banker's hand). In order to win, your high hand must beat the house's high hand, and your second highest hand must beat the house's second highest hand. It's that straightforward. You must win *both* hands in order to collect on your wager. If both of your hands rank lower than the house's hands, you lose. If you win one hand and lose the other, the bet is a push; no money changes hands. If the hands are identical, the house wins.

As in traditional pai gow, the house takes a 5 percent commission on all winning bets.

THE RANKINGS

As we said earlier, hands in pai gow poker are ranked according to traditional poker procedures. There is, however, one exception. In traditional poker, the highest straight, obviously, is an ace-high straight (10-J-Q-K-A). The second highest straight is a king-high straight (9-10-J-Q-K). In pai gow poker, however, the second highest straight is an ace-low straight (A-2-3-4-5).

Always keep that in mind. It could mean the difference between winning and losing.

The order of hands in pai gow poker, from highest to lowest:

1) Five Aces (including Joker)
2) Royal Flush
3) Straight Flush
4) Four of a Kind
5) Full House
6) Flush
7) Straight
8) Three of a Kind
9) Two Pairs
10) One Pair
11) High Card

CHAPTER 5

BACCARAT

James Bond's Favorite

Among the most elegant and exciting casino games is baccarat (pronounced BAH-kuh-rah). Long favored by high rollers and sophisticates (including Ian Fleming's superspy, James Bond, who helped introduce the game to a mass audience in the book *Casino Royale* in 1953), baccarat is a French variation on the Italian game of *baccara*, which means "zero." The name stems from the value of all face cards in the game: zero.

Casinos have traditionally tried to attract players by giving the impression that baccarat is an exclusive, glamorous game. Tables are placed in a roped-off area separate from the main casino; dealers are dressed in tuxedos; table minimums are often quite high—$20 to $2,000 being typical.

Don't be intimidated. Baccarat is actually one of the simplest of casino games, and everyone is welcome to play.

The roots of baccarat can be traced back as far as 15th-century France, although it was not widely played until the 17th century, during the reign of Louis XIV. Subsequent monarchs occasionally banned the playing of baccarat, and all gambling was prohibited in France from 1837 to 1907. At that point, with the resurrection of casinos in such places as Monte Carlo and Cannes, baccarat became wildly popular.

Bearing the nickname "shimmy," the game traveled (illegally, of course) to the United States in the 1920s; another variation was introduced in the 1950s, when gambling was legalized in Nevada. At the time, baccarat, as played in American casinos, was actually closer in spirit to the European cousin of baccarat—chemin de fer. The primary difference between the two games is this: In chemin de fer, each participant has a chance to hold the bank and compete against the other players at the table; in baccarat, the house holds the bank and competes directly against all participants at the table, whether they bet on the bank or the player (and, because the bank hand always has a slight mathematical advantage over the player hand, the casino takes a 5 percent commission on all winning bets placed on the bank).

Baccarat, as it is played in Caesars Palace and other modern American casinos, is more closely related to blackjack.

HOW TO PLAY: AMERICAN STYLE

While chemin de fer is similar in competitive spirit to poker, baccarat, as it is played in Caesars Palace and other modern American casinos, is more closely related to blackjack. In fact, some people consider baccarat to be blackjack with a European flavor. Instead of 21, however, the winning hand is the one that totals closest to 9. And, unlike blackjack, there are few options for the player in baccarat. Specific rules dictate the course of each hand. This makes baccarat an easy game to play (just put up your money, place a bet on the bank or the player and hang on for the ride), but it can be a difficult game to understand. If you become confused, don't worry. All plays are predetermined by the rules, and the dealer will explain precisely what happened on each hand.

THE TABLE

The baccarat table resembles nothing so much as an hourglass: a rectangle with indentations on the side and semicircles at both ends. Typically, the game consists of three dealers, two sitting behind the bankroll and one standing opposite the bankroll. These dealers handle bets, collect losses and pay winnings. On the other side of the table is the "stickman" or "caller," who runs the game by supervising action, determining whether a hand must take a hit or stand, and announcing the totals of all hands. The baccarat table accommodates as many as 14 players; chairs are positioned around the semicircles at each end of the table. Since seating has no effect on play, players can sit in any seat they choose.

At each end of the table, arranged in a semicircle, are seven large numbers—each corresponding to a player (13, as you might expect, is omitted). Inside the semicircle of player numbers are three more semicircles: the largest containing the word P-L-A-Y-E-R-S; the next containing the word B-A-N-K-E-R-S; and the last repeating the player numbers. Finally, in the center of this last semicircle is a small space marked with "Tie" and "9 for 1." Bets are made by placing chips on one of the three areas. In other words, you are betting on one of the following outcomes: The player will win; the bank will win; or there will be a tie. If you are sitting in seat number 1, and you wish to bet on the bank, you put your chips on the corresponding bank letter: in this

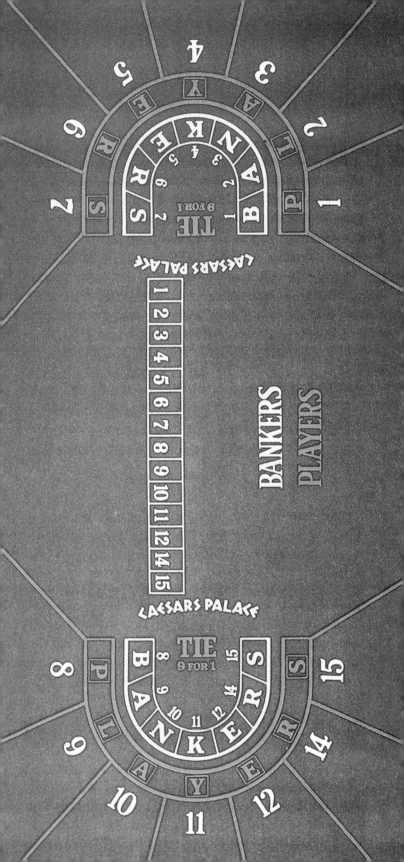

case, the letter B. If you are in seat number 2, you put your chips on the letter A, and so on. Similarly, if you are in seat number 1, and you wish to bet on the player, you place your chips on the letter P.

The words "Players" and "Bankers" also appear in the middle of the table. The dealers place the cards in these two areas, one hand representing the player's hand and the other the banker's. A series of boxes bears the numbers 1 through 15 (again, 13 is omitted). Each box represents a player and is reserved for the commission that must be paid on a hand in which the player wins by betting on the bank. For example, if you are seated in position number 1, and you win $100 by betting on the bank, you would owe the casino a commission of $5; hence, a $5 marker would be placed in the box marked "1." Commissions are not collected after each hand; rather, they are payable whenever the dealer reshuffles for the next series of games, or when a player leaves the table.

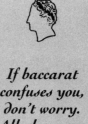

If baccarat confuses you, don't worry. All plays are predetermined by the rules, and the dealer will explain precisely what happened on each hand.

OBJECT OF THE GAME

No matter how many participants sit at the table, only two hands are dealt in baccarat: one to the banker and one to the player. Each hand begins with two cards. The object of the game is to be dealt or to draw a perfect hand—one worth nine points. Once you get the hang of it, scoring is relatively simple. All cards, ace through 9, are worth their face value. In other words, the ace of spades is worth one point, the 2 of hearts is worth two, the 3 of diamonds is worth three, etc. The 10, jack, queen and king are worth zero points. To determine the value of a single hand, just add the points represented by the cards. If the total is greater than 10, drop the first digit, and use only the digit in the ones column.

The baccarat table accommodates as many as 14 players; chairs are positioned around the semicircles at each end of the table. Since seating has no effect on play, players can sit in any seat they choose.

Example: If you are dealt a 7 and a 4, the point total of your hand is 11. Therefore, the hand is worth one point. If you receive a king and a queen, the hand is worth zero. If you are dealt a 6 and a 9, the total is 15, and the hand is worth five points. If you are dealt a 3 and a king, and then draw a 6, the total is nine—precisely the score you hope to achieve!

Baccarat moves quickly. A given hand can never contain more than three cards. And, often, the game does not go beyond the initial deal. If the first two cards you receive total nine points (a 7 and a 2, for instance), you have what is known in the parlance of the game as a "natural." Two cards worth a total of eight points is the second best possible hand and is also considered a natural. If both hands total eight, or both hands total nine, the higher of the two naturals wins. In the case of ties, neither bank nor player wins; however, anyone else at the table who is brave enough to gamble on the likelihood of a tie (which pays off at 8-1 odds), wins big.

THE RULES

Baccarat does not become complex until the two competitors begin drawing cards, which happens only when either of the hands equals a point total other than eight or nine. At that time, the rules of play—which are printed in chart form on cards available at every table—are consulted. It is here that the novice baccarat player is likely to get lost, for the hand will be played out according to the rules, regardless of your knowledge of the game.

This doesn't mean you're in danger of making a mistake that can cost you a pile of money. In baccarat, there are virtually no decisions beyond the placing of a bet. Failure to understand the rules can result in bewilderment, and it can take some of the pleasure out of the game. But you won't be punished for it. The caller simply announces the situation and the appropriate rule, and you will either win or lose. Our advice: Hang around, watch a few hands, and you'll soon feel like a pro.

In the meantime, though, here are the basic guidelines that govern the course of play and determine when the player or banker must draw a third card. As in blackjack, the player examines his cards first. Unlike blackjack, the player wastes no time fretting and fussing over whether to take a "hit." The rules of baccarat take this decision out of his control. If the player's hand totals zero to five points, he must draw an additional card (unless the bank holds a natural, in which case the player loses immediately). If the hand is worth six or seven points, the player stands. And, of course, if the hand is worth eight or nine points (a natural), the player also stands. In chart form, the player's rules look like this (keep in mind that although the chart includes the number 10, 10 really means "0"):

Player's Rules
(Note: The number 10 really means "0.")

Having	
1-2-3-4-5-10	**Must Draw a Card**
6-7	**Must Stand**
8-9	**Natural, Stands**

Whether the banker draws a third card is a far more complex matter and is at least partly determined by the third card drawn by the player. Although the rules do not state this clearly, the banker will always draw on 0, 1 or 2 (again, unless the player has a natural, in which case the game ends immediately). And the banker will always stand on a hand that totals seven, eight or nine points. If, however, the banker's hand totals three, four, five or six points, things begin to get interesting—or confusing, depending on your familiarity with the game.

Banker's Rules

Having	Draws When Giving	Does Not Draw When Giving
3	1-2-3-4-5-6-7-9-10	8
4	2-3-4-5-6-7	1-8-9-10
5	4-5-6-7	1-2-3-8-9-10
6	6-7	1-2-3-4-5-8-9-10
7	Stands	
8-9	Natural, Stands	

To read this chart, you must understand that the term "giving" really means that the *player* drew that card. For example, if the chart indicates that the banker "gave" a 3, it really means that his opponent, the player, drew a 3 on his third card. In other words, according to the chart, if the banker's hand totals three, four, five or six points, the determining factor for whether he draws a card is the player's third card. Unfortunately, what the chart does not explain is that if the player did not draw a third card, the banker draws anyway.

Confusing? At first, yes, but not after you've played for a while. Let's examine a few sample hands.

Hand Number 1
Player hand: king-4 = 4
Banker hand: 5-10 = 5

Action begins with the player. By consulting the rules of the chart, we see that the player must take a card. Let's say the player draws an 8. He now holds king-4-8—a total of two. Sorry. Bad hand.

The banker plays next. With a 5, according to the rules of play, the banker does not draw a card when "giving" an 8. Translation: The banker does not draw a third card when the player's third card is an 8. So, the banker stands with a point total of five.

Final outcome of hand: Banker wins, 5-2.

Hand Number 2
Player hand: 8-queen = 8
Banker hand: 5-2 = 7

In this case, the player has an 8, a natural. The player wins automatically. Remember, when one of the two competitors, the bank or the player, is dealt a natural, the game ends immediately and no more cards are drawn.

Hand Number 3
Player hand: ace-4 = 5
Banker hand: 3-ace = 4

The player in this situation would probably like to hold (and take his chances on the bank drawing a strong third card). This, however, is not blackjack; it is baccarat, and the player holding a hand with a point value of five has no option other than to take a hit. Let's say he draws a 7. His hand is now ace-4-7 = 2.

Now it is the banker's turn. By consulting the rules, we see that the banker, when holding a hand with a point total of four, must draw a card when the player's third card is a 7. Let's say the banker draws an 8. He now holds 3-ace-8 = 2.

Final outcome of hand: 2-2, a tie. Participants who have bet on the player or the banker get their money back; anyone prescient enough to have gambled on a tie wins—at 8-1 odds!

THE DEAL

Everything about baccarat is unique. Even the preparation of the game is dramatic: eight decks elaborately shuffled, mixed, cut and reshuffled by all three dealers—and then presented to one of the players to be ceremoniously cut. To cut the cards, the player inserts a colored plastic card somewhere in the meat of the deck. The dealers then place all eight decks into a shoe and proceed to "burn off" a few cards from the top. (The number of cards burned off is determined by the value of the first card turned over; if the card is an eight, for instance, the dealer will burn off eight cards and discard them through a slot in the table.)

In baccarat, you are betting on one of the following outcomes: The player will win; the bank will win; or there will be a tie.

Now the real fun begins.

Many players like baccarat because it is a simple game with few decisions; and yet, it is also a game that involves the players in a very direct way—more so than many other casino games. For example, after the cards are shuffled, one of the casino employees working the table will slide the shoe to the player seated in space number 1. That player is given the option to deal the first game. Let's say you are that player. You are not obligated to deal; if you feel nervous, simply slide the shoe to the next player, and concentrate on placing your bet. If, however, you crave more action, then by all means, feel free to deal!

At this point, the caller will instruct all participants to place their bets. Your first obligation here is to bet on either the banker or the player (or a tie). Remember, you deal for fun; you play to win. Let's say you throw down a $25 chip on the banker. You then extract one card from the shoe. (Don't be nervous, the card will slide out easily.) The caller will then ask you for that card, which he will place, facedown, on top of the word "Player." The next card, of course, is for the banker. The caller will tell you to leave that card, facedown, beneath the shoe (or just to the side of the shoe). The third card is then dealt to the player, and the fourth is placed under the shoe, with the banker's first card.

To determine the value of a single hand, just add the points represented by the cards. If the total is greater than 10, drop the first digit, and use only the digit in the ones column.

Banker and player now each have two cards. The caller will slide the two player cards to the person who has placed the largest wager on the player. This person then has the honor of flipping over the cards. The caller will then retrieve the banker cards from the dealer; these, too, will be flipped over and placed on the word "Banker." The caller announces point values of both hands and explains the situation (who must draw, who must stand), and the game goes on. You continue to deal until the banker loses. Then you simply slide the shoe to the player seated next to you.

That's all there is to it.

As you can see, baccarat is a game steeped in ritual. As the dealer, you are not really dealing; you are merely following instructions. And though you, as the dealer, represent the bank, you are not required to bet on the banker. Atmosphere, aided by ritual, is important in baccarat. It makes the game fun!

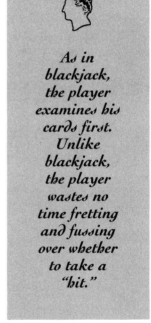

As in blackjack, the player examines his cards first. Unlike blackjack, the player wastes no time fretting and fussing over whether to take a "hit."

THE ODDS

Another reason for baccarat's soaring popularity is the likelihood of victory. Although all bets are even-money (other than a bet on a tie, which, as we have discussed, pays off at 8-1), the baccarat player stands a reasonable chance of leaving the table with more money in his pockets than he had when he arrived. The house advantage is comparatively low: 1.36 percent on wagers made on the player, and a scant 1.17 percent on wagers made on the banker. The casino extracts its 5 percent commission precisely because there is such a clear advantage to betting on the banker.

ETIQUETTE

Although baccarat is considered a glamorous game, there are no dress codes. If you have the money to play, you can find a warm and comfortable seat at the baccarat table. And just because James Bond never betrayed his emotions doesn't mean you must be overly restrained or subdued while playing. Enjoy yourself, and have fun. But keep these guidelines in mind.

• Know the parameters of your table. Tossing a $5 chip onto a table that has a $20 minimum isn't fatal, but it can be embarrassing.

• Let the caller run the game. If, at any point, you are confused, simply ask for help. It is the caller's job to make sure that the game moves smoothly.

• If you're winning, feel free to tip the dealers. It's perfectly appropriate.

• If you'd like a copy of the rules, just ask one of the dealers. Printed charts are available at every table.

CHAPTER 6
BLACKJACK
Skill vs. Chance

Blackjack is the most popular table game at Caesars Palace, and it's not hard to understand why. First of all, you have a reasonable chance of winning (for a skilled player, the house advantage can be as low as 0.2 percent to 5.9 percent, the smallest of any casino game). Second, it is a game steeped in tradition, with a romantic, back-alley image reflected in its Runyonesque language (accepting a card is known as "taking a hit") and no-nonsense hand gestures. Part of the fun of blackjack is that everyone who sits at the table feels like a big-time player—no matter how small the wager.

In many ways, blackjack is a quintessentially American game: It is fast-paced, challenging and competitive. And for the player who is both accomplished and bold, it can reap enormous rewards.

THE HISTORY

Much ink has been spilled in the debate over the origins of blackjack. At one time or another, Italy, Spain and France have each claimed paternity. Most gaming historians acknowledge a direct link between blackjack and the French game vingt-et-un ("21"). And, in fact, many people still refer to blackjack as "21." The reason, of course, is that the object of the game is to use the cards you are dealt to achieve a point value of 21.

According to *Scarne's Guide to Casino Gambling*, players of "21" began referring to the game as "blackjack" around 1912. At that time, in the Midwest, a variation of the game had started to appear with some regularity. Previously an even-money game, "21" now offered a player 3-2 odds if he reached 21 with his first two cards. Moreover, if the two-card

21 consisted of the ace of spades and either the jack of spades or the jack of clubs (all black cards), the player received a bonus of $5 for every 50 cents he had wagered.

This was an enormous enticement, and before long, this version of "21" had become more popular than its predecessor. Regular players began tinkering with the language of the game, adopting a lingo all their own, and soon the term "blackjack" was adopted to distinguish traditional "21" from the newer, more lucrative two-card variety.

It is a game steeped in tradition, with a romantic, back-alley image reflected in its Runyonesque language (accepting a card is known as "taking a hit") and no-nonsense hand gestures.

The growth of black-jack was slow during the 1920s and 1930s; most gamblers still preferred craps, horse racing and various types of poker. During World War II, however, black-jack was immensely popular with American GIs looking for a way to pass the time. When thousands of servicemen returned home after the war, blackjack's popularity exploded. By 1948, it was the most widely played casino card game in the United States.

HOW TO PLAY

The object of blackjack is to have the total point value of the cards dealt to you exceed the point value of the dealer's hand—without going over 21. If you do go over 21 (known as "busting"), your hand breaks, and you automatically lose—even if the dealer subsequently busts, as well. Most cards in blackjack take their numerical value (in other words, the 3 of diamonds is worth three points, the 4 of clubs is worth four points, etc.). An exception is the ace, which can be worth either one point or 11 points, depending on your preference (if using the ace as 11 will cause you to bust, of course, the dealer will automatically count it as one point). Face cards are all worth 10 points.

Like baccarat, blackjack is played with multiple decks of 52 cards shuffled together and placed in a shoe. You, as the player, compete only against the house, which is represented by the dealer; you never compete against the other players at your table. After shuffling the deck, the dealer will offer one of the players a plastic card to "cut" the deck. If you are offered the "cut," simply insert it halfway into the deck. The dealer will cut the deck at that position and place it in the shoe. The dealer then "burns" one card off the top of the deck and puts it into a discard pile. The purpose of this tactic, obviously, is to make it more difficult to keep track of which cards have been dealt. Typically, the dealer will reshuffle and recut the deck when he reaches the plastic card stop.

Before distributing cards, the dealer will call for bets. He starts the game by dealing one card, faceup, to each player, and a card to himself, facedown. He then deals a second card to each player—again, faceup. His second card is dealt facedown and placed beneath the first card, which is then flipped over for the players to see.

At this point, blackjack gets really interesting, for it is here that the player must make decisions that will affect the outcome of the game. Whereas in baccarat (another game in which the player tries to use his cards to reach a specific point total) every move is determined by house rules, in blackjack, the player plots his own course of action. He knows that the dealer must abide by house rules (which we'll detail), but he does not know how strong a hand the dealer really has. Beneath that face card might be an ace (a "blackjack" and an automatic winner) or a 5 (a total of 15, which constitutes just about the worst hand a dealer can have). So, before proceeding, the player must assess the strength of his own hand and compare it with what he knows about the dealer's hand.

It's one of the most fascinating, tension-filled moments in the casino, and it's what makes blackjack so special.

If you think your hand is strong enough to beat the dealer's hand, you will elect to "stand." You can communicate this to the dealer with a hand gesture: simply hold out your hand, palm down, and wave it over your cards in a negative fashion. This tells the dealer that you do not want another card.

If, after assessing your hand, you come to the conclusion that you'll need more cards in order to beat the dealer, you can ask for a "hit." Two gestures are widely recognized for this request: Tap your index finger gently on the table, very close to your cards, or cup your hand and brush your fingers along the surface of the table toward you. Either gesture will signal to the dealer your desire for another card. (If the casino is noisy, the dealer might not hear you correctly and may misinterpret your request.)

You are allowed to take as many cards as

you like, so long as you do not exceed 21. Stop (or "stand") when you are satisfied that you have achieved the strongest hand possible—given the circumstances. For example, if the dealer is showing an ace or a face card, you must presume that he is likely to end up with a reasonably strong hand. If you are dealt

a 9 and a 3, your total is 12. Under these circumstances, you should always ask for another card. Using the hand gestures described above, you would ask the dealer for a hit. In this case, the card you want is another 9, which would give you a total of 21. A face card would give you 22 points—in other words, a bust.

If you request an additional card and you bust, you lose immediately. The dealer will sweep your cards and chips from the table and proceed to the next player. When all of the players have completed their hands, the dealer will check his hand. He will often do this rather theatrically, peeking first, then flipping the card over so that all of the players at the table receive the news—whether it be good, bad or indifferent—at the same time.

By now, you've probably figured out that the dealer's hand is the center of the blackjack universe. The dealer has two distinct advantages in this game: He is allowed to keep one card concealed, and he is the last person to play his hand. Let's use the same hands we discussed above as an example. You've been dealt a 9 and a 3, for a total of 12; the dealer shows an ace. If you draw another 3, suddenly you have a hand worth 15 points. You must then decide whether you think 15 is strong enough to beat the dealer. In some cases, it will be. But since the dealer is showing an ace, you'll probably elect to take another card; at that point, you stand a reasonable chance of busting.

In many ways, blackjack is a quintessentially American game: It is fast-paced, challenging and competitive. And for the player who is both accomplished and bold, it can reap enormous rewards.

The dealer, of course, can see the value of each player's hand, so he is allowed no discretion when it comes to drawing cards. House rules clearly state that the dealer must take a hit if his hand totals 16 points or less; he must stand if his hand totals 17 points or more. If the dealer's point total exceeds 21, he busts, and all of the players at the table (excluding those who have not already busted) are winners. Otherwise, the dealer compares his hand with each player's hand. He collects from those players holding weaker hands, and pays those holding stronger hands. When the point total of your hand is equal to that of the dealer's, the bet is a push (a tie), and no money exchanges hands.

All winning bets, with a single exception, are paid at 1-1 odds. If your initial two cards total 21—any ace in combination with a 10, jack, queen or king— you have blackjack. A winning blackjack hand is paid at 3-2 odds. If the dealer also has blackjack, the game is a push, and no money changes hands. Keep in mind that blackjack always beats a multicard combination with a

Regular players began tinkering with the language of the game, adopting a lingo all their own, and soon the term "blackjack" was adopted to distinguish traditional "21" from the newer, more lucrative two-card variety.

point total of 21. So, if you are dealt a 10 and an ace, and the dealer subsequently manages to reach 21 by taking one or more hits on his original hand, you still win. And you will be paid at 3-2.

STRATEGIES AND SYSTEMS

Once you've found a seat at a blackjack table with a palatable minimum wager (minimum bets range from $5 to $25), you must devise a plan of attack. For the novice blackjack player, that means using a combination of restraint, intuition and plain old common sense. Together, these elements form the backbone of what is generally referred to as basic strategy.

When employing basic blackjack strategy, you follow a series of guidelines that will help you determine when to take a hit and when to stand. None of these guidelines is foolproof, of course; the fact that the dealer has one card hidden always lends an element of risk to the proceedings. But many experienced blackjack players believe that basic strategy is the safest and most sensible approach to the game; as a novice, you'd be well advised to become familiar with it. At the core of basic strategy is the understanding (sometimes lost in the heat of combat) that the true object of blackjack is not to reach 21, but simply to defeat the dealer.

Following are two basic strategy charts: The first assumes that the player has not been dealt an ace, which, as we've noted, is the wild card of blackjack; the second chart assumes the player has been dealt an ace.

Basic Strategy Chart 1

Player's Total	Dealer's First Card	Strategy
17-20	Any card	Stand
14-16	7-10 or ace	Hit
14-16	2-6	Stand
13	7-10 or ace	Hit
13	2-6	Stand
12	7-10 or ace	Hit
12	4-6	Stand
12	2 or 3	Hit

Basic Strategy Chart 2

Player's Total (Ace and...)	Dealer's First Card	Strategy
2-5	2-3, 7-10, ace	Hit
2-5	4-6	Double Down
6	2-6	Double Down
6	7-10 or ace	Hit
7	2, 7-8, ace	Stand
7	9-10	Hit
7	3-6	Double Down
8	Any card	Stand
9	Any card	Stand

You've no doubt noticed from the second chart that there is a term we haven't yet covered: "Double Down." In fact, it's true that in blackjack you may find yourself in a situation that calls for some action beyond simply standing or taking a hit. For those occasions, blackjack offers four unique propositions that give you an opportunity based on the strength or weakness of your hand to modify your original wager.

Surrender: Each player has the option to "surrender" (or give up) *after* receiving his first two cards. If you surrender your cards, half of your original wager will immediately be collected by the dealer.

Insurance: If the dealer's faceup card is an ace, and you believe the dealer has blackjack, you are allowed to take out "insurance" after the initial deal. The insurance bet is really just a side bet that the dealer has blackjack. In other words, you are betting that the dealer's second card will be a 10, jack, queen or king. You are allowed to wager up to half of your original bet on an insurance bet. Insurance bets pay 2-1 if the dealer does indeed have blackjack. If the dealer does not have blackjack, you lose the side bet.

Splitting pairs: If your first two cards match—say, for example, that you are dealt a pair of 9s—you have the option of splitting them into two hands. The bet on the second hand must be equal to the bet on the original hand. And you are allowed to play the second hand only after the first hand has been completed; you cannot alternate hits. A few other rules apply as well: A split hand can be split up to four times; if you split aces, you are allowed to draw only one card on each hand.

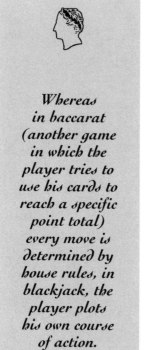

Whereas in baccarat (another game in which the player tries to use his cards to reach a specific point total) every move is determined by house rules, in blackjack, the player plots his own course of action.

Knowing when to split your cards is an important part of the game. Generally, you should follow these guidelines: Never split face cards or 10s, and always split aces.

Doubling down: After receiving your first two cards, or the first two cards of any split pair (except blackjack), you can wager an additional amount. The only stipulation is that the additional amount not exceed the value of the original bet. In other words, if you have a $5 chip on the table, and you are dealt a 5 and a 6 (for a total of 11), you may want to "double down." But the ceiling on your total wager is $10. If you decide to double down, the dealer will allow you only one additional card.

Doubling down obviously gives you an opportunity to take advantage of a strong hand. Because cards with a value of 10 are the most common cards in the deck, you should consider doubling down whenever you have a hand that totals 10 or 11—depending on what card the dealer is showing. Obviously, it's never a good idea to double down when the dealer has an ace or a face card showing.

BLACKJACK ETIQUETTE

• Always use hand signals when telling the dealer that you want to stand or take a hit. The dealers have been trained to read these signals. Decisions to split pairs, double down or take insurance, however, should be indicated verbally.

• In some casinos, the cards are dealt facedown in blackjack, and you hold your hand. But whenever the cards are dealt faceup, the player should never touch them. The dealer is the only person allowed to remove or alter the location of the cards.

• Feel free to take your time when counting the point total of your hand. Yes, blackjack is a fast game, but there is no rule to prevent you from moving at your own pace. Try not to bring the game to a standstill, however. One suggestion: Always count an ace as one point, and then add 10. And try not to worry too much. After a few hands, you'll be up to speed.

• Before you sit down and place a bet, make sure you know the table minimum (the smallest bet required to play the game). It will be clearly posted at the table.

• Never touch your chips once you have placed your wager. Fumbling with chips is a fairly common nervous habit, but save it for the chips that aren't involved in the current hand. Otherwise, the dealer might think you're trying to cheat.

• If you've had a run of luck, feel free to tip the dealer, especially if he has been polite and cooperative.

CHAPTER 7
CARIBBEAN
STUD
POKER
Progressive Payoffs

Caribbean stud is one of the newer and more popular forms of poker played at Caesars Palace. Actually, it isn't really poker at all—at least not in the strict sense of the word. Caribbean stud (the name stems largely from its popularity among guests at Caribbean resorts and on cruise ships) is a fun, eclectic game that blends elements of blackjack, video poker, slots and traditional poker.

Strange, you say? Well, yes, but this potentially awkward and confusing combination works well in Caribbean stud. The game is not terribly complex, and the payoffs, thanks to a progressive twist (therein lies the philosophical connection to slot machines), can be enormous.

Too good to be true? Just check out the Caribbean stud tables the next time you visit a casino. Chances are, the joint will be jumping.

Caribbean stud is a fun, eclectic game that blends elements of blackjack, video poker, slots and traditional poker.

HOW TO PLAY

Caribbean stud is played on a special semicircular table. Shaped much like a blackjack table, it has room for a dealer on one side and several players on the other. As in blackjack, the players compete against the dealer rather than against each other (as they would in poker). Printed on the table, in front of the dealer, are the words "Dealer Only Plays With Ace/King or Higher." This refers to the quality of the dealer's hand, and is the first of many ways in which Caribbean stud reflects the spirit of poker—five-card stud in particular.

Before the game begins, each player places his first bet, known as an "ante," on the appropriately marked space on the table. After all bets are placed, the dealer will distribute five cards to each player— including himself. All cards are dealt face-down. After the cards are dealt, the dealer will flip over his last card, revealing it to the other players at the table.

If you think your hand is strong enough to win, and you wish to continue playing, you must make a second wager (known as a "call bet") equal to twice the amount of your original ante.

If you're playing Caribbean stud, this is the point at which the game becomes interesting. It's also the point at which you must know a little bit about the basics of poker to understand what's going on, because hands are ranked according to traditional poker rankings. You must assess your cards—much as you would in any other game of poker—and determine whether you are willing to stay in the game. This decision will be based not only on the strength of your own hand but also on the one card shown by the dealer. If you have little confidence in your hand (or little money in your wallet), you may want to "fold." If so, simply toss your cards down on the table. You will automatically forfeit your ante, and the game will continue without you.

If, however, you think your hand is strong

enough to win, and you wish to continue playing, you must make a second wager (known as a "call bet") equal to *twice* the amount of your original ante. In other words, if you put up a $5 chip to start the hand, you must now put in an additional $10 to complete the hand. So your total wager is $15. To avoid any confusion, there are separate places on the table (clearly marked) for each of these wagers. Make sure you do not lump your bets together.

After all wagers are down, the dealer will reveal his cards. For the game to continue, he must have at least an "ace/king high." If he does not, then the game ends immediately, and all players who chose not to fold are automatically paid even money on their ante bet only. (If you know nothing about poker, this might sound confusing. The dealer is not required to have, specifically, one ace and one king; but his hand must have a ranking that is at *least* that high. One pair, two pairs, three of a kind—all are ranked higher than an ace/king high.)

If the dealer's hand does meet the minimum requirements, then his hand is compared with the other players' hands. If your hand beats the dealer's, then your ante is paid even money, and your call bet is paid off according to a predetermined scale of odds (which should be printed on or near the table). In other words, you'll receive more money for a flush than you will for two pairs, just as you would if you were playing video poker.

Caribbean Stud Payoff Chart

One Pair or Less 1-1
Two Pairs 2-1
Three of a Kind 3-1
Straight 4-1
Flush 5-1
Full House 7-1
Four of a Kind 20-1
Straight Flush 50-1
Royal Flush 100-1

HITTING THE JACKPOT

What distinguishes Caribbean stud from other table games is its progressive jackpot. You can make (or lose) a significant amount of money just by playing standard Caribbean stud; the progressive option, though, is the dangling carrot that makes the game truly interesting. It works like this: Before each hand is dealt, you'll have a chance to make another wager in addition to your ante. This bet (usually $1) is placed in a separate slot on the table, and makes you eligible for a separate progressive jackpot. The amount you win depends on the size of the jackpot—which varies from hand to hand—and the number of players who win on any given hand. The jackpots, of course,

If the dealer's hand does meet the minimum requirements, then his hand is compared with the other players' hands. If your hand beats the dealer's, then your ante is returned.

continue to grow until someone wins, which is why they're called "progressive" jackpots.

Progressive payoff charts vary; typically, a flush returns $50 (on a $1 bet), a full house $100 and a four of a kind $200. The biggest returns are reserved for a straight flush and a royal flush, both of which pay a percentage of the total jackpot—which, in some cases, represents a pool of money accumulated at several tables connected electronically. This method of determining jackpots is no different from the method used in progressive slots. Of course, the odds against being dealt a royal flush are extreme. Still, who isn't interested in betting a buck or two, when the potential payoff is tens of thousands of dollars? And remember, the progressive bet is merely a side bet. If you want to play straight Caribbean stud poker, go right ahead.

But don't blame us when you draw that straight flush and discover you're ineligible for the jackpot.

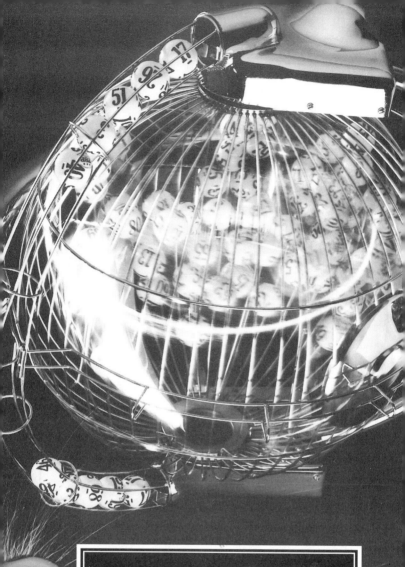

CHAPTER 8
KENO
Fun for All

One of the oldest games known to man, keno has experienced an incredible revival in recent years. Not so long ago it was in a steady state of decline at most casinos. Indeed, if you wanted to play keno, you often had to settle for the video version. No longer. Today, keno is riding a wave of popularity. Huge keno lounges, with comfortable upholstered chairs, can be found in most casinos, including Caesars Palace. Keno runners dash about, picking up tickets in lobbies and restaurants—wherever players can be found—and generally making life easier for the players. Video monitors displaying winning numbers for the most recent rounds are placed not only within the confines of the keno parlor but also throughout the casino.

The reason for this surge of interest? Keno, like its relatives, bingo and Lotto, is a simple, fun game with the potential for enormous payoffs (a $5 bet can yield as much as $100,000). Just choose a number (or numbers), place your bet and wait for the winning numbers to be selected.

You can sit in the keno lounge, fists stuffed with tickets, and watch each winning number as it is posted; or, you can fill out a card, grab a bite to eat and catch the results on a monitor.

And yet, you don't have to be totally absorbed by the game to enjoy it. The pace of keno makes it attractive to both devotees and hobbyists looking for nothing more than an interesting side game. You can sit in the keno lounge, fists stuffed with tickets, and watch each winning number as it is posted; or, you can fill out a card, grab a bite to eat and catch the results on a monitor. You can even enjoy keno while you're playing another game, such as blackjack or craps. It's that easy—and that convenient.

THE HISTORY

Like bingo, keno is a variation on *Lo Giuoco del Lotto*, the Italian national lottery. But its roots can be traced back more than two thousand years to the Han dynasty of China. Invented by a man named Cheung Leung, it was designed with a specific intent: to raise money for the Chinese army. It was popular almost from the outset—so popular that it not only helped outfit the state's soldiers, but it also provided funding for the construction of the Great Wall of China!

In its earliest forms, keno was played with 120 different Chinese ideographic characters taken from *The Thousand Character Book*, written by Confucius. Over time, the number of characters in the game was reduced to 90, and keno was played in this fashion for several centuries. By the time it reached the shores of the United States in the 1800s (when thousands of Asian immigrants came seeking employment on the burgeoning American railroad system), the number of characters had been reduced again—this time to 80, the number played today.

By the turn of the century, keno was an immensely popular (though illegal) game not only within the growing Chinese community but also with working-class people of all nationalities. The potential to win thousands of dollars on a single, small wager was thrilling—particularly to laborers, farmers and other lower-income earners. Still, there was a problem. The game, after all, was played with Chinese characters, and since few Americans could read or speak Chinese, they had to seek help in order to determine whether they had won or lost. So, eventually, the Chinese characters were replaced by the Arabic numerals 1 through 80. When that happened, of course, keno became much more accessible, and when Nevada legalized gambling, Americans made keno one of the most popular games.

Keno, as originally played in U.S. casinos, was known as "racehorse keno" because each ball also bore the name of a racehorse. Numbers were printed on small wooden balls, which were mixed by hand and then put into play through a device known as a "keno goose." The keno goose was a long tube that resembled a goose's neck. The balls would slide through the tube, and the game's director would announce the winning numbers. Today, the game is played with Ping-Pong balls stirred by air and forced

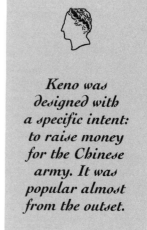

Keno was designed with a specific intent: to raise money for the Chinese army. It was popular almost from the outset.

through a pair of plastic tubes. (The device is similar to those used in state lotteries.) There are numbers on the balls but no racehorse names. And the game is known simply as keno.

HOW TO PLAY

On the surface, keno is an incredibly simple

Five Number Ticket

Six ways to make six

One way to make nine

game. The player's objective is to select anywhere from one to 20 numbers from the ticket's 80 possibilities. Keno is similar to bingo in that numbers are randomly selected to determine a winner, but the game also bears a strong resemblance to exotic wagering in horse racing because many possible combinations of bets can be made in each game. In keno, players compete against the house, which serves as the banker. Payoffs are determined by how many winning numbers you have selected on your ticket, and how much you were willing to wager.

Keno tickets (or "blanks") can be picked up almost anywhere in the casino, but they are most readily available in the keno lounge. Each ticket features two large boxes of numbers: 1 through 40 on the top, 41 through 80 on the bottom. To make your selections, just use the crayons that are provided with the blanks. Make a large X through the numbers you want to choose—remember, you must pick at least one number and not more than 20. Then decide how much you want to wager, write that amount in the space provided (it's clearly marked) and turn your ticket in to a keno writer (located at any of the cashier windows in the keno lounge). The keno writer records your bet, keeps the original ticket and gives you a copy. Your duplicate will include not only a record of your wager but also additional information, such as the date and time of the game.

REMEMBER! Hang on to your copy—you'll need it to collect your winnings. And make sure that you're aware of the time when numbers are scheduled to be drawn. Keno moves slowly, and you don't have to pay close attention, as you would at the blackjack table. But you can't afford to fall asleep, either. Keno is a seemingly endless game. Drawings are held throughout the day and night. But there is one thing you must understand: You have a limited amount of time in which to cash your ticket. Casinos will pay off on winning bets only until the next game begins.

Confused? Compare keno with a day at the races. Let's say you've picked the exacta in the second race. You now hold a winning ticket, and you have all day to get to the window to cash your ticket; in fact, you could even come back the next day, or mail it in later. But if horse racing were governed by the rules of keno, you would have only until the start of the third race to cash your winning ticket from the second race.

After that, the ticket would be worthless. So, if you're at the slot machines (or otherwise occupied) when the numbers are drawn and you discover that you have a winning ticket, head for the keno lounge! Or, if you prefer, simply flag down a keno runner and ask the runner to cash the ticket for you.

A brochure detailing the rules and regulations governing the current keno game, as well as a payout schedule for all of the different betting levels based on the number of spots you've marked on your card, is available in the keno lounge.

Caesars Palace also offers advance game keno, which allows you to play several games (five to 20) in advance—all on a single keno ticket. Simply tell the keno runner or writer that you want to play a multiple advance ticket. At the conclusion of the last game selected, you must claim your winnings from all of the games played. On 21- to 1,000-game multigame tickets, you have a full year to collect your winnings.

THAT'S THE TICKET

The interesting thing about keno is its wide range of betting opportunities. You can play one game or 100 games on a single ticket. You can combine selections in an infinite number of ways. And you can wager as little as 10 cents or as much as several hundred dollars. Be conservative or adventurous. It's all up to you. Before you begin, though, you should become familiar with the various types of keno tickets.

Straight tickets: The easiest to mark and play, a straight (or "basic") ticket is one on which the player simply chooses a minimum of one and maximum of 20 numbers. To play a straight ticket, just pick your favorite numbers (or "spots," as they're also called) and mark them with an *X* on the keno ticket. When you buy a straight ticket, you'll notice that it carries a betting minimum. You are not, however, limited to that figure. The casino will gladly accept bets in multiples of that number, and pay off according to a fixed schedule. Let's say you wager $1 on a 10-spot keno ticket, and six of

The game was played with Chinese characters, and since few Americans could read or speak Chinese, they had to seek help in order to determine whether they had won or lost. So, eventually, the Chinese characters were replaced by the Arabic numerals 1 through 80.

your numbers come up. The return on your investment might be $20 (this is just an example; always check the current payout schedule before you begin play). On a $3 bet, though, the same 10-spot ticket would be worth $60!

Just as the payoffs increase dramatically with each correct number selected, the jackpot rises with the amount of your wager. Bet $5 on a 10-spot ticket and hit nine of those numbers, and you can expect to take home as much as $20,000!

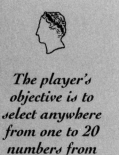

The player's objective is to select anywhere from one to 20 numbers from the ticket's 80 possibilities.

Split tickets: The split ticket, in which the player bets on combinations of numbers, is one of the most popular approaches to keno. To play a split ticket, you mark a typical keno ticket just as you would a straight ticket, drawing a large *X* through one to 20 different numbers. With a split ticket, though, that is just the first step. The next step is to circle groups of numbers that you want to play in combination.

For example, let's say you mark 10 spots, using the numbers 1 through 5 and 46 through 50. To play a split ticket, you might circle the first five numbers, as well as the second five. Or, if you prefer, you can use a crayon to draw a straight line separating the two different groups of numbers. In this case, that might make the most sense since the first five numbers are located in the upper box and the second five numbers are located in the lower box. On the side of the ticket, you would place a fraction—in this case 2/5—to explain your bet. The 2 refers to the number of bets being made, and the 5 refers to the number of spots marked in each combination. On the side of the ticket, you must also clearly note the amount you wish to bet on each combination; the total amount wagered is written in the space at the top of the ticket labeled "Mark Price Here."

So, if you wanted to bet $10 on each of the five-number combinations, you would write "$10" on the side of the ticket, near "2/5." And the total amount wagered would be $20.

Obviously, this particular split ticket is really nothing more than a pair of straight tickets. The split ticket merely allows you to save time.

Way tickets: In the language of the casino, a "way" is simply a combination of numbers. The split ticket referred to above represents two different ways to hit five numbers. A way ticket is simply an extension of the split ticket, on which the player has marked at least three equal groups of numbers; each group combines with the other groups to form several straight-ticket combinations.

The duplicate ticket issued by the keno writer will include not only a record of your wager but also additional information, such as the date and time of the game.

To play a way ticket, you might circle three different combinations of numbers, with

five numbers in each group. For example: 1 through 5; 26 through 30; and 76 through 80 (the numbers, of course, do not have to be sequential; we're using consecutive numbers for the sake of simplicity). In this case, the fraction indicating your play would be 3/10. The 3 represents the number of bets being made; the 10 represents the number of spots being played in each bet. A $5 bet on each combination would result, of course, in a total wager of $15.

Combination tickets: A combination ticket represents a far more complicated method of playing keno. When playing a combination ticket, you can combine various groups of numbers to create some elaborate bets. The possibilities are almost limitless, but let's use the three-way 10-spot ticket as a fairly simple example. If you were to combine the three 10-spots with one 15-spot ticket (remember, you've circled a total of 15 spots), you would have a combination ticket representing a total of four bets. On the side of the ticket you would now write two fractions: 3/10 and 1/15. And the total wagered would be $20, instead of $15.

As you might imagine, combination tickets can be incredibly complex. Once you understand the game, though, you'll probably want to experiment.

King tickets: The most complicated—and expensive—keno ticket is the king ticket. Simply put, the king ticket includes at least one circled number played in combination with at least two other groups of circled numbers. For example, let's use the number 3 as our "king." If we also circle two different groups, with three numbers in each group, we would have a

If horse racing were governed by the rules of keno, you would have only until the start of the third race to cash your winning ticket from the second race.

total of seven spots marked. On the side of the card, we would write the following fractions: 1/7 (representing one seven-spot combination) and 2/4 (representing two four-spot combinations). The total number of wagers is three.

Obviously, if we add another single circled number (another king), the number of combinations would increase dramatically. If you want to play a king ticket, go ahead—but give yourself adequate time to figure out all of the possible combinations. It's easy to make a mistake when filling out a king ticket.

Special tickets: Most casinos offer special keno games, featuring special types of tickets. At Caesars Palace, for example, two of the favorites are Caesars Sweet Sixteen Spot (in which the player who picks 16 numbers correctly receives $100,000 for a $5 wager) and Ten-Cent Keno (in which players have an opportunity to pick 190 combinations of eight numbers for only $19.80).

THE ODDS

Keno is a game of chance. Whether you win or lose is merely a matter of luck. You control nothing more than the amount you wager. You should also know that the house holds a substantial edge in keno—anywhere from 25 to 35 percent, depending on the type of bet you place and the amount of money being paid out on a winning ticket.

Nevertheless, keno is an enormously popular game, and it's easy to see why. It's simple and relatively inexpensive, and the return on a modest investment can be enormous. A $3 bet on a 10-spot ticket can be worth as much as $50,000 if you hit all 10 numbers. The odds against such a feat, however, are staggering: nearly 9 million to 1.

But it is the *possibility* of a windfall that draws people to keno. The jackpot in a typical game is attractive enough. What makes keno really special, though, are the progressive jackpots. It's not unusual for several games to pass without a win; and when that happens, the pot keeps getting bigger!

CHAPTER 9
BIG SIX
Wheel of Fortune

If you've ever been to a county fair or a carnival, chances are you've encountered a game of chance called the "wheel of fortune." Sometimes it's referred to as the "money wheel." At Caesars Palace, and at many other casinos, it's known as "Big Six."

The popularity of Big Six stems largely from the fact that there is truly no easier game to play in all of Las Vegas. Big Six is like a simplified version of roulette— which really isn't all that difficult to understand, either. The object of the game: Guess where the wheel will stop. If you're right, you win. If you're wrong, you lose. It's that straightforward.

For the player looking for a fast, easy game, and the possibility of a big return on a small investment, Big Six is an intriguing option.

Of course, just because you understand the game doesn't guarantee that you'll strip the money wheel of its money. There tends to be a direct relationship between the simplicity of a casino game and the likelihood of victory. The more complex the game and the more skill involved, the smaller the house advantage. Big Six offers potentially big payoffs for a small investment. But the odds against winning are steep: The house advantage ranges from 11 to 24 percent, making it one of the casino's biggest, and surest, winners.

Still, for the player looking for a fast, easy game, and the possibility of a big return on a small investment, Big Six offers an intriguing option.

HOW TO PLAY

There are 54 spaces on the Big Six wheel. Fifty-two of the spaces are festooned with the symbols of U.S. currency; two of the spaces are assigned to "house markers" (sometimes

referred to as "jokers"). The wheel is roughly five feet in diameter. Small pegs or spokes separate the spaces on the wheel. Hanging above it is a plastic or leather flap. When the wheel is spun, the spokes hit the flap, causing a loud, rapid clicking sound. The flap, of course, causes the wheel to slow down and, eventually, stop.

In addition to the wheel, Big Six features a betting table, with symbols (dollar figures) matching the symbols on the wheels. If you're interested in playing, you simply place a chip on one of the symbols. For each particular bet, the betting layout also clearly reflects the odds, which are based on the number of times that symbol appears on the money wheel.

Typically, the Big Six wheel includes 23 spaces covered with $1 bills; a winning bet on a $1 space pays even money. There are, however, only four spaces covered with $10 bills, so that bet pays 10-1 odds. A bet on the $20 space (there are two) pays 20-1 odds. A bet on either of the house markers (and they are considered separate wagers) is the longest shot in the game and pays 40-1.

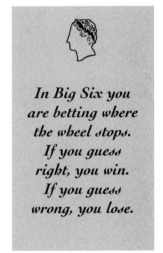

In Big Six you are betting where the wheel stops. If you guess right, you win. If you guess wrong, you lose.

Once all bets are placed, the dealer spins the wheel. When the wheel comes to a stop, the plastic stop will be clearly positioned over one of the symbols. Anyone who bets on that symbol is a winner and collects at the posted odds. Everyone else loses.

STRATEGIES AND ODDS

As we've said, the house has an enormous advantage in Big Six. And other than playing the bet with the shortest odds (the $1 symbol), there is no way to improve your chances of victory. Incidentally, to understand the degree to which the odds in Big Six are stacked in favor of the house, you need only do a little math: A bet on the $1 symbol pays even money—despite the fact that only 23 out of 54 spaces on the wheel (significantly less than 50 percent) carry the $1 symbol.

Big Six is purely a game of chance. There is no skill whatsoever involved in playing, and no proven strategy levels the playing field. It is, however, an aesthetically pleasing game sure to evoke memories of summer nights on the boardwalk or outside the big top. And for as little as a dollar, you can chase a dream.

Just don't expect to catch it.

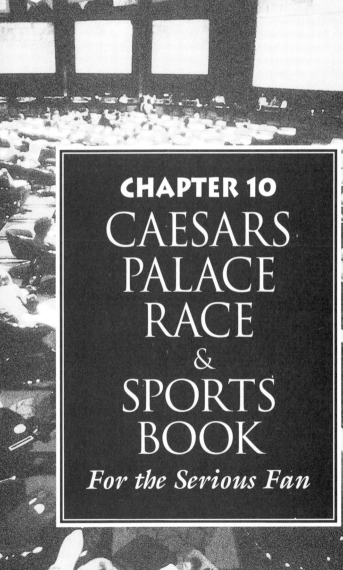

CHAPTER 10
CAESARS PALACE RACE & SPORTS BOOK
For the Serious Fan

From the gladiators who battled to the death in the time of Caesar to the modern-day boxers who wage war at Caesars, from chariot races in ancient Rome to harness races at Saratoga, as long as there have been sporting events, people have been betting on the outcome. For some, it is nothing more than a way to ensure a rooting interest in a game, a fight or a race. How common, after all, is the employee who neither gambles nor follows basketball, but is all too eager to dig into his wallet when the inevitable NCAA basketball pool begins circulating in March? Or the football widow who curses the game 364 days a year, only to find herself making a casual wager with a next-door neighbor in the middle of a raucous Super Bowl party?

For others, though, betting on athletic contests is a more serious endeavor. And it is for these people that the sports book exists. Despite cries of protest from the owners of professional sports franchises, league presidents, university administrators and coaches at the professional and intercollegiate levels, betting on sporting events remains very big business. Much of it, of course, is underground business, directed by bookmakers large and small. But legal sports gambling, too, has experienced phenomenal growth in recent years.

The betting line is nothing more than a tool used by the sports book to handicap the differences among competitors.

Publicly, the czars of professional sports leagues—the NFL in particular—express only contempt for the bettor, but they know the truth: Gambling fuels their game. Newspapers print betting lines; commentators on television pregame shows discuss point spreads and predict which teams will cover those point spreads and which will not.

Anytime betting action is not equally distributed on both sides of a contest, the line will be adjusted.

Argue the ethics of the issue all you like. The fact of the matter is, sports and gambling are inextricably linked. When people have a vested interest in a game, they're more likely to watch it on television; they're more likely to buy magazines and newspapers offering accounts of that game. The franchise owners know this. So do the media moguls who broadcast the games. And so do the advertisers who pay hundreds of thousands of dollars for a 30-second TV spot during the biggest events.

None of this has been lost on the casino industry, which, in the past two decades, has gone to great lengths to better serve its burgeoning sports-betting clientele. Once routinely ghettoized, the sports book of the 1990s is attractive, comfortable, convenient and, most important, *busy!* A stroll through the Caesars Palace Race and Sports Book at Caesars Palace, for example, offers visitors a dizzying array of gaming and entertainment options: live-satellite horse racing and daily broadcasts—on giant viewing screens—of athletic events from around the globe, computer-generated betting information updated every second, plush theater-type chairs and adjoining snack and beverage bars.

Whether you want to watch a few innings of baseball between sessions at the blackjack table or bet the entire card at Santa Anita, the Caesars Palace Race and Sports Book is the place to be. If you're a novice, there are a few things you should know before venturing into any sports book. This chapter will walk you through the basics—from point spreads and parlays to underdogs and the under/over. After all, you can't tell the players without a program.

THE BETTING LINE

It takes a combination of analytical skill and luck to predict the winner of a sporting event. But in some cases, the contestants are so thoroughly mismatched that a rank amateur could place a winning bet. That's why we have the betting line.

The betting line is nothing more than a tool used by the sports book to handicap the differences among competitors. In some sports (baseball, boxing and horse racing), the betting line is represented by odds. In other sports (football and basketball are the most obvious

The betting line does not really reflect the abilities of the teams or players involved. It simply reflects the amount of money being wagered on a particular side.

examples), it is represented by a point spread. In either case, the casino's intent is clear: to level the playing field.

Remember, the casino merely wants to take in as much money as possible, preferably with an equal amount wagered on both sides of a given issue. That way, the house maintains its edge, just as it does in every other casino game. This advantage, sometimes referred to as "juice," is ensured through various means, which we'll discuss. The thing to keep in mind, though, is this: The casino is not in the business of placing bets. The casino merely takes bets. You are the gambler. The casino is a money manager, carefully assessing all action and market fluctuations. That is why the betting line sometimes moves—not because some "expert" believes one team really has a better chance of beating the other team by a given number of points, but because money is pouring in on a particular team. Anytime betting action is not equally distributed on both sides of a contest, the line will be adjusted; if the pendulum swings too far in the other direction, it will be adjusted again.

In football and basketball, the betting line will typically read as follows: the favorite, followed by the point spread, followed by the underdog; the home team is usually in capital letters.

The line, then, does not really reflect the abilities of the teams or players involved. It simply reflects the amount of money being wagered on a particular side. For example, if Team A is a six-point favorite over Team B, it does not mean that Team A is actually six points better than Team B. That, of course, has not been determined. As long as the spread remains at six points, it simply means that the betting population as a group seems to believe six points is an appropriate spread—because its members are covering both sides of the issue in approximately equal proportions.

As we've said, the betting line is typically represented in one of two ways: a point spread or odds. Let's take a look at each.

THE POINT SPREAD

Picking the outcome of a game between a football team with a 10-0 record and a team with a 0-10 record would be an easy task—were it not for the point spread. As any sports gambler knows, the point spread is the great equalizer. Each sports book has its own odds-makers, so the point spread at one casino may differ from the point spread at another. You may be wondering how this could happen. The answer is simple: Remember, betting lines fluctuate depending on how much money is being wagered on each team. If the sports book at one casino is handling a large percentage of bets on Team A, it may adjust the line in favor of Team B; if the sports book at another casino is handling a large percentage of money on Team B, it will adjust its line in favor of Team A.

Betting on a football or basketball game is a fairly simple matter—once you understand the point spread. Let's say, for example, that the Dallas Cowboys are playing the New York Giants in East Rutherford, New Jersey (where the Giants play their home games). In the morning newspaper, the Cowboys are listed as a nine-point favorite. You see this information and decide you want to place a bet on the Giants (maybe you're from New York or maybe you just think nine points is too generous a spread). The first thing you should do is visit the sports book and check the line as it appears there. If it is still nine points, and you're still comfortable with the spread, then place your bet, sit back and enjoy the game (Sunday afternoon is just about the best time at a sports book, with virtually every NFL game available through satellite transmission).

In bets placed on football and basketball games (and anything else involving a point spread), all wagers are placed at 11-10 odds. Regardless of which team you select—favorite or underdog—you must risk $11 to win $10.

If you take the Giants, a loss is not necessarily a loss. In order to win your bet, the Giants must beat the spread. In other words, if the Cowboys win by a score of 23-15 (an eight-point margin), you win! A Dallas victory of less than nine points translates into a victory for anyone who bet on New York. On the other hand, if the final score is Dallas 23, New York 13, then you lose your bet. Any Dallas victory of more than nine points translates to a loss for anyone who bet on New York. If the final score is 23-14—a spread of exactly nine points—then the bet is a push (a tie), and no money changes hands. In football and basketball, the betting line will typically read as follows: the favorite, followed by the point spread, followed by the underdog; the home team is usually in capital letters. For example:

Dallas   9   NEW YORK

or...

Cowboys   9   GIANTS

or...

(–9) Cowboys vs. GIANTS

The "minus 9" in parentheses, of course, refers to the nine-point spread. It means the Cowboys are "giving nine points" to the Giants. A person who bets on the Cowboys, when asked which team he has in the game, would probably say, "Cowboys, minus 9," or "Cowboys, giving 9." A person who bets on the Giants would say, "Giants, plus 9," or "Giants, getting 9."

Some people are thrown off by fractional spreads, such as:

Dallas   8½   NEW YORK

Don't be confused. This simply means the oddsmakers have determined that a nine-point spread would result in too much money being bet on the Giants, while an eight-point spread would result in too much money being bet on the Cowboys. So, the spread lands in the middle. In this case, an eight-point Dallas victory translates into victory for anyone who bet on the Giants, while a nine-point Dallas victory translates into victory for anyone who bet on the Cowboys.

Point spread juice: The house advantage in bets placed on football and basketball games (and anything else involving a point spread) is established by requiring all wagers to be placed at 11-10 odds. Regardless of which team you select—favorite or underdog—you must risk $11 to win $10. If you want to win $100, you have to put up $110; if you want to win $1,000, you have to put up $1,100. To avoid confusion, it's recommended that you place your bets in multiples of these odds.

Taking this stipulation into consideration, it's easy to see how the house wins money on sports betting. Assuming that an equal number of bettors chooses Team A and Team B—and that all bettors have wagered the same amount of money—the house breaks even. Right? Wrong. Remember, the house pays $10 on a winning $10 bet; but it collects $11 on a losing $10 bet. This gives the house a 4 percent advantage—certainly not insurmountable, but significant.

THE ODDS

Betting on baseball (and other contests in which the betting line is represented by odds) is a slightly more complicated matter than betting on football or basketball. Rather than handicapping teams according to scoring potential, in baseball betting, teams are handicapped according to the likelihood of their winning. The margin of victory is irrelevant; if you bet on a team, and that team wins, you cash your ticket.

Reading and understanding the betting line on a baseball game can be a bit confusing.

After a few plays, however, you'll get the hang of it.

Let's say the New York Yankees are playing the Detroit Tigers. The morning line lists the Yankees as 8-5 favorites. This means an $8 bet on the Yankees returns $5. Similarly, if you want to win $50 by betting on the Yankees, you'd have to put up $80. In a typical sports book, however, the numbers displayed are usually based on a theoretical $100 bet. So, if the Yankees are 8-5 favorites, the number 160 (without dollar signs) would be placed next to the team's name. This means you'd have to wager $160 dollars on the Yankees in order to collect $100.

Confusing? Then forget about the odds and approach it this way: When you walk into the sports book and look at the betting lines, simply move the decimal point two places to the left, and add a dollar sign. Thus, 160 becomes $1.60. You now know that if you want to bet on that particular team, you'll have to wager $1.60 for every dollar you hope to win.

In betting on baseball (and other contests in which the betting line is represented by odds), the margin of victory is irrelevant; if you bet on a team, and that team wins, you cash your ticket.

The odds and the juice: We've told you how to bet on a favorite. But what if you want to bet on the underdog? Let's use the scenario listed above. Someone with a mathematical mind might think that you'd only have to put up $1 to win $1.60 if you place a bet on the Tigers. That, after all, would be logical. But if that were the case, the house would have no advantage; in the long run, in fact, the casino might lose more than it wins. And, of course, that is not something the casino would, or could, tolerate.

So, to ensure a profit, a house advantage is built in by fixing the odds in such a way that the benefit of betting on the underdog is never quite as obvious as the risk of betting on the favorite. Say you want to bet on the Tigers. Rather than give you $1.60 for a $1 bet, the sports book is more likely to give you $1.50. On the board, this game might read as follows:

(–160) YANKEES vs. Tigers (+150)

This advantage, small as it is, adds up over time. The juice keeps the sports book in business, and makes the game just a little more challenging to the bettor.

SIDE BETS

So far we've described only straight betting (choosing the winner or loser) on athletic events. Most casinos, though, offer a wide variety of betting options that can make for a fascinating day at the sports book. Here are just a few:

Over/under: The over/under bet is a great way to ensure interest in a game, even when the outcome has been determined. It works like this: The casino's oddsmakers establish a "line" on the game. The line is simply a set number of points. If the combined score of the two teams exceeds that number, then anyone who placed a bet on "over" wins. If the combined score is below that number, anyone betting the "under" wins.

For example, the New York Jets are playing the Miami Dolphins. The over/under is 47. You examine the teams' histories, their scoring potential and their defenses, and you determine that both teams are likely to put a lot of points on the board. So you bet the "over." The Dolphins win by a score of 32-28. The total is 60. You win your bet. If the point total is less than 47, you lose your bet. If the final score is 24-23 (exactly 47 points), the bet is a push, and your money is returned.

Parlays: A parlay, considered by many serious gamblers to be a "sucker" bet, is merely a way to combine two or more bets. The more bets you make, the higher the odds, and the greater the jackpot. Hitting a parlay, though, is difficult. Even experienced gamblers have trouble winning more than half their bets against the point spread; to win a parlay, you can't afford to have even one losing selection.

But there are benefits to parlays, the most

In the over/under bet, the casino's oddsmakers establish a "line" on the game—a set number of points—and if the combined score of the two teams exceeds that number, then anyone who has placed a bet on "over" wins; if the combined score is below that number, anyone betting the "under" wins.

obvious being that, like the lottery or keno or playing the slots, a small investment can reap huge rewards.

Future bets: If your objective is to bet on a game that you can watch on television a few minutes later, the sports book will certainly meet your needs. But there are other possibilities: the "future bet," for example. At the beginning of any season (NHL, NFL, NBA, college football, college basketball, etc.), each casino will establish odds against a given team winning a championship. Place a bet before the season opens, and follow your team throughout the course of the year. The future bet is not a practical bet; in fact, it's often a sentimental bet (on a hometown favorite or an alma mater). But if you're looking for a long shot, keep it in mind.

HORSE RACING

The Caesars Palace Race and Sports Book also features wagering on horse racing (thoroughbred and harness) and greyhound racing from tracks around the country.

Volumes have been written on the subject of handicapping the ponies—a fascinating and brutally complex science that has captivated gamblers for centuries—and we won't attempt to distill that information in this space. The wisdom you bring to the racetrack or the OTB parlor will suffice at a sports book. The rules are essentially the same. Any bet you can make at a track—win, place, show; quiniela; daily double; exacta; trifecta; pick-six—you can make at a sports book.

The horses are on the track! Good luck.

CHAPTER 11
VIDEO POKER
The Latest Craze

The computerized version of America's most famous card game has something for everyone. Combining a high degree of both skill and luck, video poker is a fast, enthralling game offering some of the best odds of any gambling machine. For the novice and the expert, the objective is the same: to assemble the best possible five-card hand.

PURIST'S PLEASURE: THE HISTORY OF POKER

Poker is the real deal—gambling for grownups. Its roots can be traced back many centuries, to an ancient Persian card game called *as nas*, in which players made bets on who would have the highest-ranking combination of cards. It also bears a resemblance to the French games *Bouilotte* and *Ambigu*. At its heart, though, poker is a profoundly American game, one that champions such traits as fierce individualism, bravery and ingenuity. It is an exciting, challenging game that is not for the timid or faint-hearted.

Although surely a derivation of other types of card games, the poker we recognize today was actually born in the United States in the early 19th century, and is generally believed to have been adapted by the Cajun population of Louisiana. The Cajuns, descendants of French explorers who settled in the Mississippi Bayou region, referred to the game as poque, which was probably derived from the French word *pocher*, meaning "to bluff." Not everyone, though, ascribes to that theory. The late John Scarne, one of the world's greatest gambling experts and historians, believed that the word "poker" stemmed from the colloquial term "poke," which thieves and pickpockets used to describe a wallet. Why? Because in its infancy poker was considered by elitists to be less a game of skill than a game of deception; and, in fact, floating poker games were, as often as not, populated by cheaters and scam artists.

Nevertheless, poker gained an enormous following among riverboat gamblers on the Mississippi. Never had they seen a game that presented such a unique challenge and offered such large rewards. To that point, card gambling had largely been an impersonal exercise in which players competed against a "bank" in games such as "faro," much as they do today in blackjack or baccarat. With the introduction of poker, however, the gambler's world changed. Suddenly he found himself seated at a table, competing against the players to his right and left. This added a psychological dimension rarely, if ever, encountered when playing against a bank. The bank was cold, unyielding, distant. It made no decisions; it simply followed the rules.

In poker, though, the rules were merely guidelines. They provided a blueprint for the way in which the game would proceed. But within that blueprint were myriad possibilities. The poker player needed more than just luck. He needed knowledge, skill, strategy… *strength!* He needed the courage to bluff his way into a large pot, and the good sense to fold when loss was inevitable. Like no card game before it, poker was about competition.

It helped, of course, that poker also held the promise of great wealth. Bank games typically involved a single wager; poker allowed for several wagers. In a very real sense, the sky was the limit. For the high-stakes gambler, poker was nothing less than the elixir of life. No wonder, then, that the game migrated quickly across the Great Plains and into the Rocky Mountains. It became a fixture at taverns and saloons throughout the West. Some games were clean, some were dirty, and pity the poor fool who stumbled upon the wrong table. Then, as now, there was an inherent risk in playing poker. One was never quite sure of the abilities—or ethics—of the other players at the table. That sometimes made the game dangerous. It also made it thrilling.

Poker was, and is, gambling…in the purest sense of the word.

THE VIDEO VERSION

Not so long ago, casinos offered only a handful of options for the shy or self-conscious player, the person who longed to try his hand at poker but found the prospect of sitting down at a table and engaging in competition far too daunting to seriously consider. For those customers, the casinos offered—and still do offer—slot machines and various other games demanding little skill and virtually no social interaction; after all, to each his own.

A poker player needs the courage to bluff his way into a large pot, and the good sense to fold when loss is inevitable. Like no card game before it, poker is about competition.

The technological revolution of the past two decades, however, has opened doors for the player who wants to become acquainted with some of the more traditional and exciting table games without actually having to confront a dealer; without having to sweat over whether the guy across the poker table is bluffing; without having to worry that he'll make some silly mistake in blackjack, like splitting kings—a faux pas that's likely not only to cost him his wager, but also to lead to some serious embarrassment.

It is now possible to play poker (and many other games) in comparative solitude, in a low-pressure environment, thanks largely to devices known in the industry as "specialty machines."

The truth is this: Not everyone enjoys playing the tables...not even those who might enjoy the games that are played at the tables. If you fall into that category, fear not. For it is now possible to play poker (and many other games) in comparative solitude, in a low-pressure environment, thanks largely to devices known in the industry as "specialty machines," the most popular of which, by far, is video poker.

Video poker machines were introduced to bettors in 1976 by the Bally Manufacturing Co. Interestingly enough, the games were, at first, considered little more than a novelty and were largely ignored by the gaming public. Two years later, though, International Game Technology began competing with Bally for floor space in casinos, and soon video poker had secured a foothold in the business. Today it is one of the fastest-growing segments of the industry. Customer demand has prompted casinos across the United States to rethink floor plans and allocate more and more space to video poker (and to some of its relatives, such as video blackjack, video slots and video keno). Rarely in the history of casino gambling has a new game enjoyed such phenomenal popularity in such a short time.

The reasons for this remarkable growth are fairly obvious. Video poker gives the customer a chance to play one of the casino's most exciting games—a game of skill as well as luck—in a nonthreatening environment. Poker is perhaps the most well known card game in America; and yet, in the past, many people who visited casinos were so intimidated by the prospect of playing against strangers that they never gave the game a try. Video poker has changed all of that. It gives the casual player a chance to experiment with one of the truly great card games without having to worry about being humiliated—or worse, cleaned out—by a professional gambler. And, at the same time that it entertains and challenges the player, video poker serves as a tutorial; it will prepare you for a dose of the Real Thing, if that's what you want.

Then again, you might be perfectly content to do battle with a computer. If so, good luck. And enjoy the ride!

RANK OF HANDS

Before you play any type of poker, you should become thoroughly familiar with the rank of each hand. In video poker, as in regular poker, the rank of individual cards is from highest to lowest: ace, king, queen, jack, 10, 9, 8, 7, 6, 5, 4, 3, 2.

Easy enough, right? Understanding the rank of hands in poker is a bit more complicated. Unfortunately, there are no formulas or tricks. If you're going to play the game, you simply must commit these hands to memory.

143

Failing to do so will surely cost you money. So here they are, the rank of poker hands, in descending order (each hand in poker consists of five cards):

Royal Flush
10-J-Q-K-A (all of the same suit)

Straight Flush
Five cards of the same suit in sequence (for example: 3-4-5-6-7 of clubs)

Four of a Kind
Four cards of the same rank (for example: ace of hearts, ace of clubs, ace of diamonds and ace of spades)

Full House
Three of a kind, along with a pair (for example: three jacks and a pair of fives)

Flush
Any five cards of the same suit, but not in sequence (for example: 3 of hearts, 6 of hearts, 7 of hearts, queen of hearts, ace of hearts)

Straight
Any five cards in sequence, but not of the same suit (for example: 2 of clubs, 3 of diamonds, 4 of hearts, 5 of spades, 6 of spades)

Three of a Kind
Three cards of the same rank (for example: king of hearts, king of spades, king of clubs), along with any two other cards.

Two Pairs

Two sets of cards of the same rank (for example: 7 of hearts, 7 of spades, queen of clubs, queen of diamonds), along with any other card

One Pair

Two cards of the same rank (for example: jack of clubs, jack of hearts), along with any three other cards

No Pair

A hand with no matching cards. In this case, the value of the hand is determined by the highest card (for example: ace of hearts, 10 of diamonds, 9 of spades, 3 of spades, 2 of clubs; this hand is known as "ace high")

HOW TO PLAY

When you walk into a casino, it isn't hard to spot the video poker machines. From a distance, they will look like slot machines. And when they pay off, they will sound like slot machines. Typically, though, customers stand while playing the slots; when playing video poker, they sit in chairs. This gives the player the feeling that he is involved in a real game, one that requires concentration and skill, and not merely mindless repetition. Almost like sitting at a poker table.

The typical video poker machine has a small video screen on which the player's "cards" appear. (There are no real cards, of course, just as there is no real dealer.) Beneath the screen, or to the right of the screen, is a group of buttons. When you're ready to begin playing, you will insert a coin (or several coins, depending on the specifications of the machine, which we will discuss later). The next step is to push the button marked "Deal."

At this point, the computer that controls the machine takes over. Each hand in video poker is dealt from a new, freshly shuffled 52-card deck. Each hand consists of 10 cards. The skeptic—or the technophobe—might question the "integrity" of the dealer. After all, at least when playing real poker, you see the dealer actually cutting and shuffling the cards. In video poker, a certain leap of faith is required. But you needn't be concerned. The cards are selected by a computerized device known as a "random number generator." The same technology applies to slot machines. There is, however, a huge difference between video poker and slots. The slot machine player simply drops a coin, pulls the lever and hopes for the best. When playing video poker, you are, to a degree, at the mercy of the machine. But you have an opportunity to make choices that will undoubtedly affect the outcome of the game.

When playing real poker, you see the dealer actually cutting and shuffling the cards. In video poker, a certain leap of faith is required. The cards are selected by a computerized device known as a "random number generator."

Simply put, the difference is this: Playing the slots is passive; playing poker—even video poker—is active.

After you hit the deal button, your first five cards will appear, faceup, on the screen.

(The second group of five cards remains in the computer's system, in reserve; they will serve as replacements for the cards you have been dealt, should you choose to draw any new cards.) After you've examined your cards carefully, you will decide which cards you wish to keep and which cards you wish to discard. Beneath each of the cards in your original hand is a button. By pressing any of these buttons you are electing to "hold" that particular card (in fact, the word "Hold" will appear on the screen, above or below each of the cards you have elected to keep). So, if you want to keep two of the cards you've been dealt, and discard the other three, you simply push the buttons that correspond to the cards you'd like to keep (you may keep as many cards as you like—from one to five).

When deciding which cards to keep and which to discard, there are a few basic guidelines to follow, the most important and obvious of which is...know the odds. A foolish risk often taken by the novice poker player involves the straight. Let's say, for example, that you are dealt the 3 of clubs, 4 of hearts, 6 of diamonds, 7 of spades and ace of spades, a hand commonly referred to as an "inside straight." Your first inclination would be to discard the ace and go for the straight. The odds, however, are not in your favor. In fact, the odds against drawing a five and completing the straight are 11-1. So, unless you're feeling extraordinarily lucky, you should discard everything except the ace and take four new cards.

Following is a list of poker hands and the odds against improving them in logical fashion. Before you play, you'd be well advised to commit the odds to memory.

Video Poker: Know the Odds

Opening Hand	Cards Taken	Desired Hand	Odds
Pair	Three	Two Pairs	5-1
Pair	Three	Three of a Kind	8-1
Two Pairs	One	Full House	11-1
Three of a Kind	Two	Full House	16-1
Three of a Kind	Two	Four of a Kind	23-1
Four-card Flush	One	Flush	4-1
Two-sided Straight	One	Straight	5-1
Inside Straight	One	Straight	11-1

CHANGING YOUR MIND

After making your selections, take another hard look at the computer screen; make sure that you are comfortable with your choices. If, for any reason, you wish to change your mind (maybe you accidentally pushed the wrong button), now is the time to do it. Most video poker machines allow you to rectify mistakes by pressing a button marked "Error" or "Erase." Hitting the error button simply gives you another opportunity to make your selections; it will not void your hand, nor will it prompt the computer to deal you a new hand. If you have been dealt an extraordinarily strong hand, you may wish to keep all of your cards. In that case, simply press all five hold buttons.

Note: On some machines, you will not be asked to designate the cards you wish to keep; rather, you will be asked to select the cards you would like to discard. The procedure, however, is the same. Simply press the button corresponding to the cards you would like to throw out. The computer will automatically mark those cards. If you want to keep all of your cards, press the button marked "Stand."

After you've designated the cards you want to keep, and you're completely satisfied with your selections, it's time to ask the dealer for replacements. Press the button marked "Draw" (on many machines it's the same as the button marked "Deal"). The cards you have elected to hold will remain on the screen; those you have discarded, however, will be replaced by new cards.

Video poker is much like regular "five-card-draw" poker in that the five cards you possess after the draw represent your final hand; you are not allowed to take any more cards. Unlike live draw poker, however, there is no bluffing. If your hand is strong enough, you win. And, since you are competing against a standard (the house's fixed schedule of payoffs), rather than against another player, you'll know in advance how much each winning hand is worth.

If you have a winning hand, one of two things will happen: Either coins will drop into the well at the bottom of the machine (one of the sweetest sounds in any casino), or a credit meter on the video display will tell you how much you've won. The credit meter keeps track of your earnings as long as you play. When you're done, simply press the "Cash-out" button and wait for the coins to drop. The credit meter simplifies the game by allowing you to play without having to continually insert coins into the slot.

Video poker is the perfect game for the novice card player. Although you do need some knowledge of poker, you need not be an expert. Winning hands, with their respective payoffs, are posted near the video display. Winning at video poker is similar to winning at slots in that the more coins you insert, the more money you are paid on a winning hand. You can also become eligible for bonus payoffs by playing the maximum number of coins. For example, in video poker the payoff on a royal flush (poker's best hand) is typically 250-1. Put in one coin, draw a royal flush and the machine will return 250 coins. Two coins will pay 500 coins, three coins will pay 750 and coins will pay 1,000. If you insert a fifth coin, however, the jackpot increases dramatically, to 4,000 coins!

Following is a standard video poker payout schedule, with hands listed in descending

Video Poker Payout Schedule

Hand	1 Coin	2 Coins	3 Coins	4 Coins	5 Coins
Royal Flush	250	500	750	1,000	4,000
Straight Flush	50	100	150	200	250
Four of a Kind	25	50	75	100	125
Full House	9	18	27	36	45
Flush	6	12	18	24	30
Straight	4	8	12	16	20
Three of a Kind	3	6	9	12	15
Two Pair	2	4	6	8	10
Jacks or Better	1	2	3	4	5

order, from strongest to weakest. Remember, the payout is one coin, not one dollar. In most casinos, one hand of video poker can be played for as little as 25 cents. Some machines require at least a quarter; others require a minimum of one dollar. In either case, the minimum required to play the game is represented by the phrase "one coin."

As you can see, some hands that often reap rewards in live draw poker are considered losers in video poker—any small pair, for example. When playing video poker, always keep in mind that a pair of 10s is no better than a pair of 9s—or a pair of 3s for that matter. You need to "catch" (specialty machine jargon for getting the cards, or numbers, you want) jacks or better to win. Remember, you're playing against the machine, not another player.

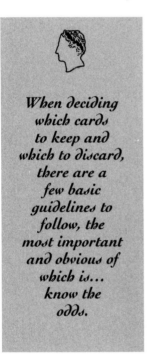

When deciding which cards to keep and which to discard, there are a few basic guidelines to follow, the most important and obvious of which is... know the odds.

You should also know that the payout schedule shown is for nonprogressive machines. Progressive machines usually feature a grand prize that continues to swell until someone hits the grand prize. Payout schedules on these two types of machines are similar, but not identical. Typically, for example, the progressive machine offers a bigger pot of gold at the end of the rainbow, but smaller rewards on some other hands, such as a full house or a flush. And, although draw poker is by far the most common type of video poker game, you might also encounter machines that offer jokers or deuces wild. Again, payout schedules on these machines will differ slightly.

VIDEO POKER STRATEGY

The trick in video poker, obviously, is knowing which cards to keep and which cards to toss aside. Because there are so many possibilities on each hand, strategy can be incredibly complicated, depending on how daring you are. The ultimate goal is a royal flush, with its attendant jackpot, but does that mean you should risk a probable straight, with its lower payoff, just to go for the big money? Should you break up a pair (and throw away the possibility of getting three of a kind or four of a kind) to go for a royal flush? Well, maybe yes, maybe no. There are no easy answers. Each situation calls for a thorough examination of the hand and wallet, coupled with—as always—common sense.

Let's say you're dealt the jack, queen and king of spades, along with the 10 of spades and 10 of hearts. You have a pair of 10s, and the possibility of drawing another 10, for three of a kind. Clearly, though, in this situation, you'll want to discard the 10 of hearts and go for the royal flush (or, as a consolation prize, a regular flush).

Then again, if you draw the jack and queen of spades, along with the 10 of hearts, 10 of spades and 10 of diamonds, you'll want to think very carefully about trying for a royal flush. After all, you already have a three of a kind—a guaranteed winner. Taking risks is half the fun of gambling, of course, but the other half is winning. There are two good rules of thumb when playing video poker:

1) Never break up a winning hand.
2) Always stand on a "pat" hand.

Sound confusing? It shouldn't. A winning hand is not necessarily a pat hand. If you have three of a kind, it's a winning hand, but it's also a hand that might be improved by taking two cards. A pat hand, though, is one that either can't be improved or might be ruined by drawing cards. The following are pat hands: a royal flush, a straight flush, four of a kind, a straight, a flush and a full house.

The possible exception to this rule is when you are only one card away from a grand prize payoff; if, for instance, you hold the king, queen, jack and 10 of clubs, along with the 9 of diamonds. This is a straight and a clear winner. However, it's also tantalizingly close to a royal flush (exchange the 9 of diamonds for the ace of clubs). And the payout on a royal flush is so large that it might be worth a try.

Then again...maybe not. It's up to you. Regardless of your approach to the game, video poker is an eager opponent.

OTHER OPTIONS

If you like the idea of playing against a computer, but poker isn't for you, Caesars Palace has several options, including:

Video blackjack: Introduced before video poker, video blackjack (or "21") is played just like live blackjack. The computer will deal two hands, one to the player and one to the dealer. Each hand consists of two cards. Both of the player's cards will be dealt faceup. One of the dealer's cards will be faceup; the other will be facedown.

As in video poker, you signal your instructions to the dealer by pressing buttons on the machine. Most video blackjack machines offer the opportunity to double down or split pairs, just as in live blackjack. The primary difference between the two games is that at blackjack the video version usually pays even money, rather than 3-2 odds. An advantage to video blackjack, however, is that you can play for smaller stakes (a dollar per hand, for example, or even less) than you can at a table version of the game.

For a more detailed explanation of blackjack, please see Chapter 6.

Video keno: Video keno, like video poker and video blackjack, requires a basic understanding of the live version of the game (a complete overview of which can be found in Chapter 8). Presuming you know how to play keno, you'll find video keno a breeze.

Most video poker machines allow you to rectify mistakes by pressing a button marked "Error" or "Erase." Hitting the error button simply gives you another opportunity to make your selections.

Eighty numbers are displayed on the video screen. The machine will clearly state the maximum amount of numbers you are permitted to select (usually 10). After you have pushed the buttons corresponding to the numbers you want, you push the "Start" button. The machine will churn for a moment, and then the winning numbers will light up. If any of the numbers you selected match the computer's numbers, you win; the more matches, the greater the payout.

THE ODDS

When deciding whether to play a live game or a video version, several factors must be taken into consideration, not the least of which is the likelihood of victory. In traditional draw poker, which relies quite heavily on skill, the odds are nearly impossible to predict. There is simply no way to know whether that woman sitting next to you is a shark or a fish until, perhaps, it's too late. In video poker, though, you know everything there is to know about the opponent. You know that the house odds vary widely (anywhere from 1 to 12 percent), depending on the skill of the player and his willingness to pursue jackpots or progressive payouts. And you get to play in solitude. If that sounds appealing, then video poker is the game for you.

In video blackjack, the house advantage is clearly greater than in table blackjack because the house does not offer 3-2 odds in the video version. And in video keno, while the odds are approximately the same, fewer, and smaller, grand prizes are available.

The bottom line: Specialty machines offer a pleasant introduction to many of the casino's most popular games in video format. They can be an enormous amount of fun. And they can be profitable. But you should also be aware of the risks and pitfalls. Remember, gambling is gambling, whether you're sitting at a table with other people or standing alone at a machine.

There's no such thing as a sure thing. It's just a matter of personal preference.

AFTERWORD

A Final Word on Gaming at Caesars Palace

Now that we've supplied you the necessary information, you'll probably want to try your hand at one of the many casino games we have to offer. Sit back, relax—this is going to be fun.

Remember, we've given you an overview of how to play the games and explained some basic strategies. The rest is up to you. Decide what game you want to play and how aggressive you plan on being. Set your limits. Know your budget for playing the games and stick to it. If you gamble with your head and not over it, you'll do just fine. You'll also have more fun.

Good luck...and let the games begin.

For Caesars Palace reservations and information, call 1-800-CAESARS.

GLOSSARY

Action: The amount of money being wagered on a game, as in "the action is good."

Ante: An initial bet put up by all players before the first card is dealt in a poker game.

Banker: Whoever covers the betting in any game, usually the casino.

Bankroll: The amount of money a player intends to gamble.

Bet the limit: The maximum amount a player can risk in any game.

Bluffing: When a poker player raises with a weak hand in an attempt to drive players with stronger hands from the game.

Burn a card: The top card (or cards) of a shuffled deck is "burned" or discarded by placing it faceup at the bottom of the deck.

Bust: In blackjack, a player busts when his cards total over 21.

Checks: A synonym for chips; tokens used in place of money in casinos.

Come-out: The first roll of the dice in craps that establishes the point.

Comp: Complimentary; casinos reward regular players or high rollers with "comps" like free or reduced meals and/or rooms.

Crapping out: Losing by rolling a 2, 3 or 12 on the come-out.

Croupier: Dealer in baccarat or roulette, from the French.

Cut: To divide a deck of cards into two or more parts, which the dealer will then put together in a new order.

Cut card: A colored card used to divide a deck.

Drop box: A locked cash box underneath a gaming table for storage of chips, markers and cash.

Even money: A bet whose odds are 1-1.

Exacta: Choosing the order in which two horses finish a race.

Face cards: In a deck of cards, any jack, queen or king.

Handicapping: Used at the sports book; figuring the odds on a horse or sports team's chance of winning.

Hit: In blackjack, to take another card.

GLOSSARY

House edge: The percentage which the casino retains in any game of chance.

Jackpot: A big win.

Keno board: The electronic board that shows winning keno numbers.

Keno runner: Employee who takes keno bets and delivers winning payments.

Line: The sports book's estimation of the odds of an individual or team winning a contest; designed to encourage betting by attracting bettors to both sides.

Marker: An IOU that the player establishes at a gaming table.

Mini-baccarat: Baccarat for lower-wagering players.

Money management: An individual player's method of controlling his bankroll; one of the most important things any player can do is manage his money carefully.

Natural: A perfect hand; in craps, a 7 or 11 on the first roll; in blackjack, an ace, with a 10, jack, queen or king; in baccarat, drawing an 8 or 9 in the first two cards.

Over: A bet at the sports book in which the bettor guesses that the combined point total of two teams will be above (or over) a specific total.

Pit: Any area of the casino where a group of tables are placed.

Pit boss: The casino employee who is the executive in charge of all personnel and games in the pit area; the job includes keeping an eye out for cheating, dispute resolution and personalized service for bettors, including comps.

Progressive slots: Any slot or group of slot machines in which the jackpot increases with each nonwinning bet.

Push: A tie between the house and a player in which no money changes hands.

Quiniela: A bet at the sports book in which you choose two horses and win if the horses finish first and second, or second and first.

Shoe: The wooden or plastic box that holds multiple decks of cards.

Shooter: Whoever is rolling the dice in craps.

Sports book: That part of the casino where all wagering on sporting events occurs.

Stand: In blackjack, when you choose not to receive additional cards.

Trifecta: In horse racing, choosing the first three horses in one race.

Under: A sports bet in which the bettor guesses that the total points scored by two teams will be under a certain figure.